GRAND CONVERSATIONS, THOUGHTFUL RESPONSES

GRAND CONVERSATIONS, THOUGHTFUL RESPONSES

A Unique Approach to Literature Circles

FAYE BROWNLIE

PORTAGE & MAIN PRESS

Portage and Main Press acknowledges the financial support of the Government of Canada through the Book Publishers Industry Development Program (BPIDP) for our publishing activities.

Printed and bound in Canada by Hignell Printing.
Designed by Relish Design Studio Ltd.

05 06 07 08 09 5 4 3 2

Library and Archives Canada Cataloguing in Publication

Brownlie, Faye
Grand conversations, thoughtful responses : a unique approach to literature circles / Faye Brownlie.

Includes bibliographical references.
ISBN 1-55379-054-5

1. Reading (Middle school)   2. Literature—Study and teaching (Middle school).   I. Title.

LB1575.B77 2005   428.4'071'2   C2005-902246-9

PORTAGE & MAIN PRESS
100-318 McDermot Avenue
Winnipeg, Manitoba, Canada R3A 0A2
Tel.: 204.987.3500

Toll free: 800.667.9673
Fax: 866.734.8477
E-mail: books@portageandmainpress.com

To Gaby, who proudly became a reader in her first encounter with literature circles. Thanks, Frankie!

CONTENTS

ACKNOWLEDGMENTS

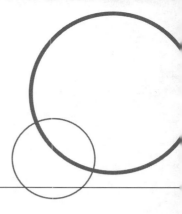

Writing about learning in classrooms is always the result of powerful collaborations. Many teachers and students enriched this journey for me. Special thanks to:

- Tait teachers Tina Pali, Laurie Laing, Garnet Millman, Myra Allan, Karen Pacheco, Simi Bains, Carole Reed, Ruth Jacobsen, and their students, for the recent literature circle explorations in their classrooms.

- Leyton Schnellert, Gordon Powell, Joanna Fournier, Judith King, Joanne Panas, Jennifer Katz, and Tina Pali, for sharing their lists of books that worked.

- Nicole Widdess, Kathy Pantaleo, Krista Ediger, Tina Pali, and Jennifer Katz, for describing examples of their work with literature circles.

- Gina Rae, Carole Saundry, Leyton Schnellert, and Judith King, for their thoughtful, reflective questioning.

- All those teachers who have written to me after workshop sessions to share their excitement and successes.

It takes a community of teachers to raise a community of readers.

INTRODUCTION

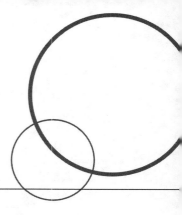

Many books have been written about literature circles, an organizational strategy whereby students read a variety of novels and have group discussions about their reading. What distinguishes the approach that I have developed and present in this book is that students have a choice in what they read and in how much they read. They are not assigned roles in their discussion groups. And they are not required to read at the same pace as the other students in their discussion group; they do not have a set number of pages or chapters to read each day. What also distinguishes this approach is that it results in stronger, more sophisticated readers. Students engage in what educational scholar Gordon Wells calls "grand conversations"; they come up with thoughtful responses, and they read and read and read some more! I believe that all students can and do become powerful, enthusiastic readers if we provide them with a choice of great books and create a flexible framework in which they can talk about the books they choose to read.

I have been developing this approach for the past fifteen years. When I began, I was working as a resource teacher in an elementary school where we were trying to increase the amount of reading done by our intermediate students. As was common practice then, we were moving away from basal readers to a combination system that included the whole class reading each novel at the same time, individualized reading (where students chose their own books, read at their own rate, and conferenced individually with the teacher) and USSR (uninterrupted, sustained, silent reading). This worked for some students. But, for others, the whole-class novel was frequently too hard for them to read independently. These students tended to engage in "fake reading" during USSR and develop extravagant avoidance strategies during individualized reading, which amounted to very little actual reading done. We were not pleased with the progress in reading of our students and knew we had to do better. We knew from the synthesis of research by Fielding and Pearson about what works in reading: that students needed ample opportunities to read, explicit teaching of comprehension strategies, opportunities for peer and collaborative learning, and conversation and writing in response to their reading. This was the birth of the version of literature circles that I present here.

During the time I've been developing this approach, I have continued to teach part-time but have also worked extensively in staff development. I have continued to refine my approach to literature circles through demonstration lessons in which teachers observe and reflect on the lessons, through ongoing workshops in which teachers work to implement the approach to literature circles with their own students, and through teaching university courses in which I listen to the voices and acknowledge the expertise of teacher-learners. I first wrote of this approach in the book I wrote in 1998 with Catherine Feniak entitled *Student Diversity,* which provides a forum for responses from experienced teachers, and I learned from these responses. What you read in *Grand Conversations, Thoughtful Responses: A Unique Approach to Literature Circles* is my current thinking on what has grown to be a powerful strategy for developing sophisticated readers, expanded now to readers in Grades 2 or 3 to Grade 12.

Over the past fifteen years, I have noticed several significant shifts in my practice and in the students' responses:

- As students gained more control over *what was read* (i.e, choosing their own books rather than me or the group determining appropriate books) and *how much was read* (i.e., students taking the books home and reading the whole book in a night if they chose to, rather than me determining how much the whole class would read), they read more.

- As I became more skilled at teaching them how to talk about books, students' conversations became more passionate and involved.

- As students became more skilled at talking about books, their conversations helped them come to new understandings about their reading (Wells's "grand conversations").

- As I became less a leader in the group and more an equal participant, students assumed the leadership role and were able to talk about what really mattered to them.

- As I reinforced the need that all voices be heard in the group, verbal students began to specifically ask questions of the quieter students, while the quieter students took more seriously their need to contribute to the conversation.

- As I became more explicit in my teaching of response writing, the students became more reflective and more able to write about their thinking about the books.

I was on my way to developing readers who read avidly. This approach is possible in today's inclusive classrooms. The format of openness allows everyone to participate in a meaningful way. Our classrooms need to be communities of learners where all belong. These are the classrooms described in this book.

HOW DOES MY APPROACH TO LITERATURE CIRCLES WORK?

There are several key components to the design of my approach to literature circles:

- A collection of books is made available for the class. In choosing these books, the teacher aims to have about six different titles and five or six copies of each title for a class of thirty. More books need to be available in the collection than there are students in the class; as students will not necessarily be exchanging books at the same time, surplus books need to be available. Within the book collection, there needs to be a title choice that is both readable (at an appropriate reading level) and desirable (something that students will want to read) for each student in the class. And the number of available copies of each title is important. If you had only three copies of a particular title, for example, when the students came together in their discussion group (the group is defined by the students reading a particular book), the group would be too small. Conversely, if you had nine copies of a title, this discussion group would be too large for all participants to have a chance to talk.

- Students meet in discussion groups, twice a week, to talk about the book they are currently reading. The discussion group is made up of all students who are reading the same book at any given time.

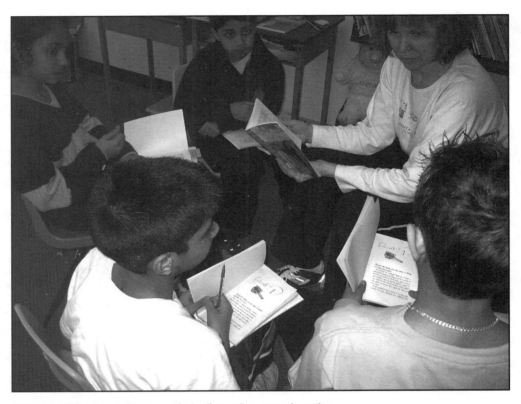

ILLUSTRATION 0.1 A literature circle discussion group in action.

A teacher generally joins the discussion group. While the discussion is going on, the other students in the class are reading other books. Because students can read at their own rate, when they meet to discuss the book, they will all be at different parts of the book. Students are encouraged to "tease" other readers (i.e., to encourage them to read on) but not to "spill the beans" about the book.

- Students come to the discussion with a passage from the book that they would like to read aloud as a conversation starter. Other students in the group respond to the conversation starter (the Say Something strategy). The discussion lasts fifteen to twenty minutes.

- As students complete a novel, they return it to the collection and choose another book and join the discussion group for that book.

- Two or three times a week, students respond in journals to the books they are reading. The choice of journal format changes with the increasing skills of the students.

- Every two weeks, all students complete a comprehension activity based on the novel they have just completed reading.

- Large blocks of time (seventy-five to ninety minutes) are most effective for group discussions.

CHAPTER 1

GETTING STARTED
LEARNING THE SAY SOMETHING STRATEGY

The heart of literature circles is the discussion group. In the past, it was standard practice for teachers to assign roles to students in literature circles in order to facilitate discussion and engage all students. However, my experience shows that this can lead to rather contrived conversations and can be an organizational challenge. What inspires students toward more effective reading is the chance to talk with their classmates about what they are reading—in small groups where all voices are respected and heard and where all students are included. Furthermore, what makes these discussions in themselves effective is openness in the involvement of the students. The more choice students have in what they read and how much they read, and the more choice they have in focusing their discussions, the more effective the discussions will be.

When readers read, they are engaged in making sense of text. They enter into a contract with an author that is based on interaction. Readers know that their role is to make sense of the authors tracks— the words left on the page. The process of making sense of a text involves creating images, asking questions, making connections, drawing inferences, predicting, analyzing, sythesizing, and responding emtionally. Good readers do these processes fluidly and flexibly. Students need to be aware of the behaviors of proficient readers, to be taught these processes and encouraged to use them while they are reading.

The most effective way to facilitate discussion—to help students use their thinking—is to use the Say Something strategy (Harste, Short and Burke). This strategy involves everyone in the group and gives the students considerable control over the conversation. It is open enough that everyone can participate and no one can monopolize. Say Something is a first step on the way to teaching students to participate in thoughtful, engaging conversations about their reading.

I teach the students an adaptation of the Say Something strategy on the first day of literature circles, before the novels are even introduced. Try these steps:

1. Begin with a poem. This poem can be thematically related to the upcoming novels, or not. A short poem (one page on the overhead) works well, as it allows students to understand how much can be gleaned from so little text when they really use their images, questions, and connections.

2. Present the poem on an overhead and have one of the students read it aloud to the class while the others read it silently.

3. As the students are reading, ask them to notice their thinking about the poem—their connections, their questions, the images that emerge.

4. Conduct a class "whip around." Each person in the class says something about the poem or makes a connection to what another person has said (the Say Something strategy). The teacher makes no editorial comment but scaffolds for those students who are unsure about what to say. The teacher makes explicit the kind of "saying" that students are doing—for example, personal connections, big ideas, images, word analysis, This reminds me of..., I wonder about... These responses are examples of the thinking of good readers who understand more deeply what they are reading, who become engaged with the text. Keep in mind, and make sure that the students understand, that there is no right answer. Encourage students to notice how each person's thinking can be very different from another's thinking and how our own thinking and understanding are enriched by others'. Reinforce the idea that meaning lies in the mind of the reader.

5. ESL students and others who are severely challenged by class participation may enter the conversation by repeating what another student has said, or by simply saying "I agree." The goal is to increase all students' participation in the conversation, then move them to new understandings as a result of the conversation.

6. Practise with a second poem.

7. Remind students that what they have been practising here, the Say Something strategy, is what they will be doing in their discussion groups.

8. Emphasize how easy Say Something is, how much fun it is, how interesting it is, and how much you can be surprised about someone else's thinking.

When students, especially older students, have been working effectively with the Say Something strategy for a while in their literature circles, they become able to participate in less structured conversations. These experienced students may begin their conversation by posing questions that have come to them while reading. Alternatively, they may talk about surprising or interesting parts or read a powerful quotation from the text.

Always keep in mind the criteria for an effective group discussion:

- all voices must be included;
- all students must feel included;
- all students must have their ideas respected;
- the discussion should move us to new understandings.

CHAPTER 2

THE NOVELS

COMPILING THE BOOK COLLECTION

The quality of the novels you choose for the starter book collection is critical. Students will read widely and passionately if the novels they read are compelling. I suggest waiting until about the middle of the school year (perhaps after Christmas) before you begin literature circles so that you know your students and their reading interests well. It is very important in the preparation of the starter book collection that there be at least one book in the collection that will be a good fit for each and every student. In an inclusive classroom, there is certain to be a wide range of reading abilities among the students, and your book collection should reflect and respect this range. The more competent students will be delighted with a great collection of good books and will likely read them all. The less able readers will start with books that are comfortable for them and, as their background knowledge of the novels grows as they move through their literature circles, they will read beyond themselves.

To develop your own skill at choosing books—read, read, read! And talk with other teachers about the books that their students have devoured. Find a great library or children's bookstore, and have their staffs guide you. Most importantly, talk with your students about their reading interests, watch what they read on their own, and have them reflect on the choices in your starter book collection.

As you compile your collection, choose books with specific students in mind. Do you know their interests? Do you know what they have been reading independently? Have you talked with them about books they read last year in class?

For a class of thirty students, choose six titles and make sure that there are five or six copies of each title. Remember that each student needs a book to begin with. You also need several extra books because, as a student finishes reading one book, that book is returned to the collection and a new books is chosen. So, it is necessary to always keep a few books more than the number of students. It would be helpful to keep one extra copy of each title for yourself. You'll need these when you join the discussions and can share them should a student forget a book at home.

PRESENTING THE BOOK COLLECTION

The skill with which you present the starter book collection for literature circles is critical to students making wise choices. Consider these points in introducing your books:

- Read each book on the list before you present it to your students.
- Be enthusiastic.
- Give a quick overview of the book, including the plot, key characters, why you chose it, what caught your fancy.
- Read an excerpt from the novel so students can hear the language.
- Give a page count, comment on the esthetics (white space, illustrations).
- Remind students that the groups are fluid, so they should choose a novel that suits them personally, not a novel that will enable them to be with their friends (students will read their books at different rates from their friends and will change groups when they finish a book so will not necessarily stay with their friends).
- Present all novels before allowing students to make their selections.
- Ask students to make two choices. If their first choice is unavailable, then they are ready with a second. They will be able to read all of the novels eventually, if they so decide.

When presenting the novels, discuss the easier novels in a respectful way. Try to avoid the suggestion that a particular novel is included for reluctant or less able readers. Give the students new phrases to use, for example, phrases that avoid the connotation "easy book." I sometimes say, "This book is a good choice if you are finding that you are really busy just now [with hockey, soccer, music lessons, family commitments, for example]. You will be able to read it and not feel frustrated about how long it is taking you and how little time you have available." Conversely, if you are presenting a very challenging book, you can say, "This is a book that will require a lot of thinking [because of the multiple plot lines, for example, or the amount of background knowledge required] or a lot of time, and you may most enjoy it if you can really dig in and read for large chunks of time."

HELPING STUDENTS MAKE THEIR OWN CHOICES

Once you have presented the full range of books, the students are ready to make their choices and begin reading. Give them as much freedom as possible. Invite them in groups to come forward and pick up their books. Remind them that, if their first pick is gone, they will have a chance to read it soon.

Sometimes a less able student still makes a book choice that you feel will be impossible for him or her to read. Should this happen, discreetly hold back a copy (or use one of your teacher's copies) of one easy novel and one challenging novel. I approach one of the very able readers in the class with the challenging book and say, "When I was choosing books, I had you in mind for this book, *Camp X* (Walters), because I know how interested you are in spies. This, amazing as it sounds, is based on a true story of spies in Canada. I think it will grab you. When you have a chance, will you look at it and give me some feedback, please? You don't need to change books now, just when you have time." Then I approach the less able student and say the much same thing: "When I was choosing books, I had you in mind for *Terror in the Harbour* [McKay] because I remembered that you had relatives in Nova Scotia and thought you might like this story set in Halifax. It is based on a true and very gruesome event. I think it will grab you. When you have time, would you look at this book and give me your opinion, please? You don't need to change books now, just when you have time." I leave both students with these respective books. Students are very likely to respond to this approach because it is phrased as an invitation, and it is face-saving for the less able student. If the student wishes, he or she will return the too-challenging book and read yours. Frequently the student will say to classmates, "I need to do this for her"; this is a face-saving device and helps students acknowledge their need to be part of the team.

When you are helping students who you think might have chosen books that are too challenging, it is important to start with an able reader (or the students who see themselves as less able readers might choose books and then lie in wait for you to descend on them and remove their choice!). It is still their choice as to whether or not they want to switch books. I have often been surprised by a student's diligence with a book that I thought might be too challenging. If, after following these steps, you are still concerned about the match of a book with a student, it is time for a quick conference with the student (and it's important to do it the next day). On the third day, if it is clear that the student has made little progress with the book, I remind him or her that the goal is just to read. I suggest that this book might be a better choice later in the unit and that perhaps choosing a different book is needed now to reach the goal. It is our responsibility as teachers to ensure that each student progress and that no student be left behind, languishing with a too-challenging text and not reading.

It matters not if able students choose easy novels; they will read them quickly and move on to another choice. This adds market value to the book: students will notice that the able reader has read a book that might have had less status (i.e., perceived by some to be the easy book).

Sometimes teachers feel the need to provide boundaries for students who are less able readers, and at times for able readers too. Here are three additional ways for assisting students with book choice:

1. Have students write down their top two choices, then match the students to the novels. This supports students making independent choices but also allows some room for teacher involvement in the decision.

2. Assign one novel to a specific group or privately encourage these students to select this novel before the books are presented. You can give this group more support in reading this novel by meeting in their discussion group more often and helping them practise making explicit connections or asking questions in Say Something; having one-on-one mini-conferences to ensure comprehension or to build the background knowledge necessary to understand the novel. Once these students have completed one novel with more support, they may be able to choose their second novel independently and will likely work more successfully in a less teacher-directed situation.

3. Invite a support person (a teaching assistant, a resource teacher, or an ESL teacher) to work with a group who is working on a particular book.

ADDING TO THE STARTER BOOK COLLECTION

Some students will read all five or six titles of the starter book collection very quickly. (Reading for them is already a valuable activity, and they are usually delighted that someone has put together a collection for them!) And so you'll need to add to your list. Here are some suggestions:

- Make your first additional book one that will appeal to those students who have been reading quickly. This book may be longer or more challenging than some of the others.

- Once a book has been read by most students, remove it from the collection and add another title. Present each new book to the class as you add it to the collection and identify the book that is to be removed. Make sure, however, to give students who haven't read it once last chance to read it.

- Remove any books that are rarely chosen.

- Add books by authors who are already represented in the collection, books in a series already represented there, or books that have the same themes as those already on the list.

- It is less important now than it was at the beginning that you limit the growing collection to five or six books, as group size can be increased by inviting back students who have already read the books in the original collection.

KEEPING TRACK

Create a poster that lists the names of the students. Students fill in the title of the novel they are reading. At a glance, you can see who is currently reading which book and who has completed which books. Students tend to use this poster when choosing their books; they like to see, at a glance, who has read what. The poster will also show who needs encouragement to read more and who might be invited to return to a particular discussion group.

CHAPTER 3

THE DISCUSSION GROUPS

Most students will tell you that the discussion group is their favorite aspect of literature circles. They just love to get together and talk about books! The discussions invariably provide new insights into characters and events, spark questions that students haven't previously thought of, and provide a forum for in-depth thinking. The discussions bring forward parts of the novels that have touched students' hearts, kindled their curiosity, or invited them into new worlds. Teachers and students alike leave the discussions energized, having honed their thinking against the thinking of others. If you have been used to assigning roles to the students in your groups, you will be amazed at how effective these conversations are when you begin the discussion with a passage and use the Say Something strategy!

The discussion groups should not meet without teacher supervision, at least at first. You need to meet with each group regularly, and only one group will meet at a time. Try and meet with each group at the elementary level twice a week (less often in the higher levels). You can increase the amount of group discussion time by enlisting the help of adult support people: librarians, resource teachers, ESL teachers, teaching assistants. These support people of course need to have read the book that they are discussing. (Each support person will need to have read only one book in preparation and can move to whichever group is currently reading that book; the mix of students in the group changes while the support person remains the same.) These groups provide a great deal of information that you can use for planning future mini- and whole-class lessons in vocabulary, strategies, response, and comprehension.

ILLUSTRATION 3.1 A teacher meeting with students in a discussion group.

ILLUSTRATION 3.2 While one group meets, the other students read and respond.

18

Since you will include all students (e.g., ESL students and students with other special needs), make sure that the variety of books you put on the starter book list takes into account the reading interests and abilities of all students. You might even include picture books that provide background knowledge about the novels. Make them available for students to choose along with the novels and present them to the whole class as at the same time as you present the novels. For a student who requires extensive support, you might enlist the help of a teaching assistant to work with that student, using the picture book as the text.

Clearly identify to all students what the behaviors of sophisticated group participants would be. A sophisticated group participant:

- comes to the group with a passage to read and discuss;
- initiates conversation;
- builds on others' ideas;
- includes others in the conversation;
- listens respectfully;
- takes turns;
- makes text-to-self connections;
- makes text-to-text connections;
- makes text-to-world connections.

The more that students are aware of these expectations, the easier it is for them to practise them, resulting in a grand conversation. Students move beyond repeating what has happened in the text, to what others have said, to thoughtful conversations and new understanding.

RUNNING A DISCUSSION GROUP

You, as the teacher, are responsible for running the literature circle discussion groups. But your challenge is to participate as a group member and not to put yourself in the position of group leader and be the hub of all discussion. This is your opportunity to listen carefully, guiding the conversation only as needed, coaching the students toward independence in their discussions. Here are some suggestions:

- Ask students to come to the group with a passage to read to the others in the group. Instruct them to choose it with a specific purpose in mind; for example, it could be a funny piece, a well-written piece, a poignant piece, a confusing piece, or an exciting piece. And, since this is oral reading, ask them to practise it ahead of time.

- Have one student read a passage and explain why it was chosen. Each student in the group then responds with a comment (Say Something), confining the comment to the piece and their response to it, not the quality of the oral reading. You, as the teacher, also take a turn. Once each group member has had a turn, you can allow for free-ranging discussion.

- Students in the group will invariably be at different points in the book at any given time. Encourage them to tease and tantalize others with their conversation and their passage choices but to not "spill the beans." Students who have read less of the book are often inspired to read more quickly after a group discussion.

- Make sure the group size stays optimum: between four and seven members. Students who have completed a particular book will often request the opportunity to return to the group that is discussing that book. These participants tend to be keen and often add spirit to the discussion. But be careful not to let the group size get too large; too large a group will limit the amount of time for each student to talk.

- Meet with each discussion group for about twenty minutes. This will probably allow for only two students to read (especially if the discussion is vibrant), but all students should come prepared to read a piece.

- Your task in the group is to model appropriate group behavior and to support students in learning the behavior. When you feel they are ready, you can leave them on their own. The goal is for students to be able to conduct their own discussion, their grand conversation, creating a better understanding of the novel.

- During group discussions, the other students in the class will be reading independently, or perhaps working on their response journals and/or their comprehension strategies.

- Join the group from time to time and record your observations about student participation: who initiates a conversation; who builds on others' ideas; who includes others; who listens respectfully; who takes turns; who makes strong text-to-text, text-to-self, and text-to-world connections.

- Also record what you notice about each student's oral reading. But keep in mind that your participation is more important than on-the-spot record-keeping.

- When you are finished with one group, alert the next group as to their meeting time: "I am going to be meeting with the next group in five minutes. Please be prepared."

- Between group meetings, circulate among all students in the class to see if anyone needs help. Talk quietly with students who require more direct contact, and/or answer any questions they may have. Students quickly learn to self-monitor and read or work independently for much longer than the twenty minutes of formal group discussion.

FLUIDITY WITHIN DISCUSSION GROUPS

A critical component of these literature circles is fluidity of group membership. Unlike the more traditional method, in which students in the group read at the same pace and thus finish the book at the same time, students move to another group as they finish a book. The makeup of any particular discussion group is rarely the same for more than one or two meetings. Some students might find themselves in a new group almost every time they meet for discussion, while others might stay with the same group, depending on how long it takes them (and everyone else) to read their choices. This approach:

- gives students considerable choice in the amount of time they spend reading the books they have chosen;

- allows the students who might read a novel so quickly that they would miss the chance to meet in a discussion group when they are reading it to carry on; they can be invited into a discussion group for a book they have finished while they are in fact reading their next choice;

- allows students to stay in a particular discussion group for a long time while the others move onward; the student who stays for a

ILLUSTRATION 3.3 Older students meet simultaneously in discussion groups.

longer period of time will build up a "resident expertise," which, particularly for students who struggle with reading, can be rewarding—there can be some additional status built into this situation.

Once you feel that the students are able to meet independently, let them fly! You will be able to tell when your presence in the group is superfluous—the students will talk around you, not relying on your guidance. In my experience, however, most literature circles below Grade 8 are most effective when a teacher is present. Your own life experiences add another layer to the conversation, and students seem to appreciate this. As a teacher, I am constantly amazed at how sophisticated the conversations in discussion groups are, and at the level of learning that unfolds, that I can hardly stay away! I think it is preferable to stay too long rather than release responsibility for independent discussion too soon and run the risk of having the groups break down. Keep in mind that you are not running the group; you are a model participant!

BUILDING INDEPENDENCE IN DISCUSSION GROUP MEMBERS

The unltimate goal with literature circles is to help students engage in meaningful conversations about their novels with all the students in their group without the help of a teacher-facilitator. At first, you will find that some students will readily talk about their books with one or two others in the group, to the exclusion of the quieter students. These more verbal students need to learn how to include the quieter ones and how to not monopolize the conversation. The less verbal students need to learn how to contribute to a conversation and not let other students carry them. As soon as all the students have learned how to honor all voices in the group, they are ready to meet independently.

The Say Something strategy is a sure way of ensuring that all students have a chance to speak; they are, in fact, required to speak before the group can move to an open discussion. But, while the Say Something strategy provides a vehicle that supports all voices, it also limits a completely natural conversation, so it is important to make it clear that it is a means to an end—the end being open, natural conversation. Once students are comfortable with including everyone, they can begin their discussion without the support of Say Something. Some groups might begin with their student questions, highlights, or connections, and might even skip the reading aloud of a passage, but always having the option of returning to the text to support their comments. When groups are working independently, the same expectations apply as in Say Something: all voices must be included and students must listen respectfully to one another.

With older students who are able to work independently, several discussion groups can meet simultaneously, and the teacher can move from group to group, listening in, taking notes on student interactions, and participating as invited or needed.

CHAPTER 4

RESPONSE JOURNALS

Response journals are invaluable tools to help students become sophisticated readers. Students' reflections in response to their reading and their conversations become increasingly insightful and personal as they gain experience. Students at first are expected to record only significant aspects of the story but eventually become more adept at understanding how the text supports them in making connections—with their personal lives, within the text, and to the outside world. The act of writing helps deepen their thinking and their understanding—helps them to become more reflective readers.

Writing in response journals is not a new concept. However, too often teachers allow students to write just "the same old thing," for example, a retelling of the story (not a meaningful reflection) or a statement about how the story might remind the student of some event in his or her own life (where it's not clear whether the student has read the story or not). Some teachers have students write in response to a variety of prompts. These prompts provide more variety than "the same old thing," but they don't allow for personal meaning-making on the part of students. Prompts support dependence rather than independence.

Writing in response to reading without the goal of deeper understanding is a waste of time. What we as educators want is that their writing enable students to personalize a story and gain insights about the characters, to help them reflect, and to help them see the world in a different way.

MODELING RESPONSE JOURNALS

I believe that modeling is the most effective way to teach students the art of journal writing. Write your own journal response on an overhead,

ILLUSTRATION 4.1 Matthew working on his response journal.

explaining your thinking as you write. Have the students tell you what they notice about your process and how they will shape theirs. This analysis builds shared expectations for the task among the students and between teacher and students. It is the beginning of the criteria-building process and should be recorded as such. Once the modeling and the "notice that" stages have been completed, students can begin their own journal writing.

TYPES OF RESPONSE JOURNALS

An effective journal entry, no matter which type, artfully combines specific text reference with personal analysis. The weaving of these two elements becomes more implicit with time and practice but begins very explicitly and concretely. Your choice of journal framework needs to match your students' need for explicitness.

Begin with the end in mind—which is always to have students identify aspects of the text that are significant to them and to use these aspects (e.g., quotes, events) as a springboard for personal analytical

WHAT HAPPENED	MY THINKING

ILLUSTRATION 4.2 A typical page set-up for a double-entry journal.

thinking. When you plan with the end in mind, it will be clear which response framework is most appropriate for your class. Generally, begin with a common class journal framework rather than try to teach variations simultaneously. The double-entry journal is the basis of all my other response-journal frameworks.

Frameworks for response writing should always be elegantly simple! And the types I present here are all elegantly simple.

The Double-Entry Journal

The double-entry journal is the most common journal framework and has many variations. As presented here, the variations grow with the child. The student folds a page in half and writes about what happened in the story on the left-hand side of the page and his or her thinking on the right-hand side. The expectations for the writing on both sides of the page become more sophisticated as the students gain more experience, as is illustrated in the following graded examples. Each new framework requires more reasoning on the part of the student.

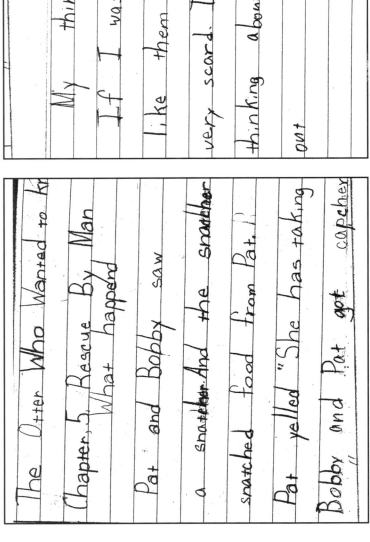

The Otter Who Wanted to K[...]

Chapter 5 Rescue By Man
What happend

Pat and Bobby saw

a snather And the snather
snatched food from Pat.

Pat yelled "She has taking

Bobby and Pat got capcher

My thinking

If I was capchered

like them I would be

very scard. I would be

thinking about getting

out

captured

ILLUSTRATION 4.3 A summary and a personal reaction written by a Grade 2 student.

Instructions for Students in Grades 2 and 3:

- Fold a page in half.

- Entitle the left-hand side What Happened and the right-hand side My Thinking or Text/Response.

- After reading, summarize what happened on the left-hand side of the page and then write your thinking about what happened on the right-hand side.

Typically, when they begin this journal, students will write more on the What Happened side than on the My Thinking side. As the balance shifts toward an equal amount of text on each side, students are ready for a shift to a different journal framework. The sample from *The Otter Who Wanted to Know* (Tomlinson) (Illus. 4.3) is typical of students writing independent responses in Grades 2 and 3. The retelling section has become more focused and the thinking is a personal reaction.

Instructions for Grade 4 and 5:

- Fold a page in half.

- Entitle the left-hand side What Happened and the right-hand side My Thinking.

- After reading, write two key events from the book on the left-hand side of the page and then write your thinking about these two events on the right-hand side.

Typically, students will write more on the What Happened side of the page than on the My Thinking side then eventually move to a more equal balance. As they become more experienced in their responses, their inferential reasoning will develop and become fuller. They are becoming ready for a more challenging response framework.

Jake's sample from *Terror in the Harbour* (McKay) (Illus. 4.4) is nicely balanced. He can identify two separate events in the book and respond with personal connections. His goal is to write fuller responses on the My Thinking side of the page. This balance is quite typical for students beginning this kind of response in Grades 4 and 5.

Instructions for Grades 6, 7, and 8:

- Fold a page in half.

- Entitle the left-hand side Quotation (Event) and the right-hand side My Thinking (My Response).

Terror in the Harbour

What happened	My Thinking
Penelope found her mothers clock face down. Penelope felt so sad and alone because her dads not there or anyone who can help her	I felt sad because the clock was the most specialist thing that reminded her of her mother and the love that she gave her
Penelope thought that she had saw Papa walking in the distance and she called his name over and over but no one answered Penelope! Someone yelled out maybe it was him it was Papa	I felt happy for Penelope because she finally found her dad. If I didn't my dad I would be crying.

ILLUSTRATION 4.4 A double-entry journal prepared by a Grade 4 student describing two events and providing two responses.

pgs. Christina	The Giver
Event	My Response
163	"That night, Jonas was forced to flee."	If I was in Jonas's shoes I'd probably be a nervous wreck. I think I could of gotten across the bridge with Gabe too. But when I had to sneak through the community, my heart would of been pounding as fast as an ink jet printer would go, printing off 20 pages a minute.
170	"A day came when the search planes did not work at all."	This small event gave me a balance of feelings. I felt sort of sad when the planes did not come at all. But I feel free at last for Jonas and Gabe. Jonas must of been in an awkward position thinking that the community most of thought he was dead or something. But it'd sure take a load off his back. If he didn't have to worry about the planes. Then he wouldn't have to transfer the cold memories to Gabe anymore.

ILLUSTRATION 4.5 A double-entry journal page written by a Grade 7 student including quotations from the text and insightful, well-developed personal responses.

- After reading, record a significant quotation (or two or three) on the left-hand side of the page, then respond to the quotation on the right-hand side.

At this grade level, we should expect that responses to the quotations will include specific references to the text personal extensions, and connections. Christina (Illus. 4.5) is able to identify three key quotations in *The Giver* (Lowry) and respond to each one with a specific reference to the text, a personal reaction, and insight about the characters. She is closely connected to her reading.

The United Journal

The united journal is most effective when used with students who have moved through the various stages of the double-entry journal and have become competent with identifying key quotations to illustrate their thinking about the book. It combines information from the text with personal reactions, in connected response. The explicitness of the "folded page" of the double-entry journal is gone. The writing moves seamlessly from text reference to personal reaction and back again. It is a reliable framework for students in the middle- and high-school years. It is a good response framework to use when student discussions are thematically based.

Model the united journal for the students by writing in front of them on the overhead or blackboard, talking about your thinking and how you construct your responses. Have students collaborate with you as you write, and invite them to analyze your writing and to begin to develop criteria for using the united journal.

When you have finished modeling, have students write their own responses to the text, making sure they connect what happened with a personal reaction.

Darren (Illus. 4.7) has used specific evidence from the text to support his belief in the power of the family in *The Old Brown Suitcase* (Boraks-Nemetz).

The Combination Journal

In the combination journal, students place sticky notes in the text to remind them of events in the book to which they want to respond. They are writing a fluid, integrated response in direct reaction to events or quotations in the text (hence the term *combination*).

Before writing in their journals, they return to the sticky notes and read around them, then choose one that sparks their thinking to begin. Students write in their journals, paying special attention to how the flagged event has caused them to think more deeply about their reading and their lives.

Mimi's response (Illus. 4.8) to *A Boy's Life* (McCammon) is the first time she has used the combination-journal response framework. Notice her inferences and personal connections.

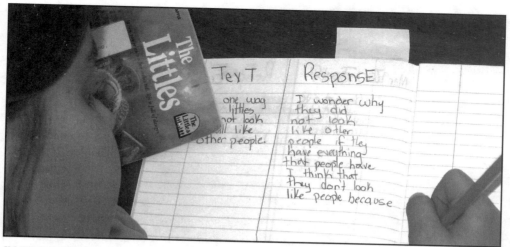

ILLUSTRATION 4.6 Shaelene working on her response journal.

POWER OF FAMILY

I can see that Slava and her father share a pretty strong bond between them. Whenever she's feeling down or something, she would go to her father for assistance, and reassurance. Like that time when they were being sent to the Ghetto and Slava slipped in, instantly her father picked her up so she wouldn't be shot. I think that I also feel more comfortable, and safe around my dad (I don't know why though…). I predict that the bond between Slava and her father will continue to grow stronger and stronger, but that relationship will be put into a test soon.

I don't really see a lot of relationship between Slava and her mom. I don't blame her mom though, she already has her hands full with the baby, and she ALSO has to tend to her husband (even though he seems to be fine, you can't skip the fact that he has a tumor in his old war wound). You can tell Slava's and her mom's relationship isn't that good because, when they decided to send Slava out of the Ghetto, her mom barely even said a good-bye. While her dad took her out, got everything set up, and gave her an official farewell hug. Unlike my family, since I'm the only child I of course get quite a bit of attention (not that its considered a good thing in MY point of view).

I predict that there will be some rough times that Slava's family will encounter. They would have to work it out as a family, stay together, and stay strong.

Darren C. *The Old Brown Suitcase* Response Journal

ILLUSTRATION 4.7 A united journal response written by a Grade 7 student that seamlessly integrates personal reactions, specific reference to the text, and thematic connections.

EVENT: THE PIANO LESSON

It turns out that Ben's taking piano lessons. From what I've seen, he hates piano, he hates his teacher and hates going to lessons, because it turns out that they will lead to him breaking their tradition.

They always went to the "Carnival" at six thirty to ten o'clock, every year. But Ben has piano, so they have to go at seven. It's not really a big deal, just a change.

I'm wondering if Ben really does have a secret love for piano, and is just too afraid to tell his friends because he'll get made fun of…I'm thinking this way because Ben's a pretty good kid, and I don't think that he would do anything to make his parents force him to sign up…If they have to pay more money for him to take lessons, then why would they anyway?

It's stupid when parents force their kids to do things because if they're not eager and willing, then they'll get frustrated and they won't try. Everyone should do what they love…

Of course, there are exceptions. Like if somebody hasn't been in any sport teams, music lessons, etc., for a long time, sometimes trying new things is a good thing to do, because you won't know if you like something until you try it.

I love basketball and I love soccer, so I signed up. It was my idea, my parents just needed to approve. I know if they forced me to take curling or something I would be really mad at them because it's not something I'd like to do.

I'm not going to mention any names, but parents shouldn't force their kids into "team" sports because if the person isn't trying because they don't like it, they're not only bringing down themselves, but they're bringing down the team. ….

Personal response to the new response format:

I found this way to respond (with the event, and then the response) helped me a lot because when I sit down to write a reading response, I usually have no idea what to write. But keeping track of the events with the sticky notes reminded me of things that I could write about, and before I knew it, I had typed out seven pages. I would enjoy responding to my book this way again, if at all possible!

ILLUSTRATION 4.8 A sophisticated response prepared by a Grade 8 student. She has used sticky notes as a starting point and successfully combined personal connections and analysis of the text. Note also the student's thoughts about using the new response framework.

The Dialogue Journal

The main point of journal writing is to clarify one's thoughts by committing one's thinking to paper. Usually journals are meant for personal reflection, but in the classroom setting they are also meant for the teacher to read. In the dialogue-journal response framework, the other reader is another student. Dialogue journals are always popular. Have students work in pairs; each of them should be reading the same novel and have reached about the same point in it. Students write a letter to their partners in response to the novel. They write this letter during class time and don't discuss their writing with each other. The following day, in class, students exchange journals and read each others' letters, then write back to their partners about the novel. Students at all grade levels respond with the same excitement to this kind of journaling. This is a letter from a friend!

I include two examples of the dialogue journal here, one from Grade 2 students, and one from Grade 7 students. Amber and Sandra are in Grade 2, and they are reading *The Missing Piece* (Silverstein). Notice how Sandra extends Amber's thinking in her response. Carrie and Melissa, in Grade 7, are reading *Cleopatra VII* (Gregory). Again, the thinking of one student plays off that of the other.

HOW OFTEN SHOULD RESPONSE JOURNALS BE USED?

Teachers frequently ask how often a response journal should be used. There is no one right answer. Some teachers have their students write, in class, each time literature circles are scheduled. Some teachers begin by having students write their responses in class, then move to journal writing as homework. Most teachers find that writing in response journals each and every day is too frequent.

Initially it is helpful to have all students write at the same time because you are modeling, building criteria, sharing responses, and building expectations. This is most easily done in a shared context: the classroom community. However, once expectations are clearly understood, students who are not meeting in a discussion group with a teacher at any given time can choose either to read or to write in their response journals. This allows them to write a response when it is particularly appropriate for them and allows them more choice and more personal control.

The sharing of journals among class members helps develop the community of readers and writers. Students enjoy exchanging journals.

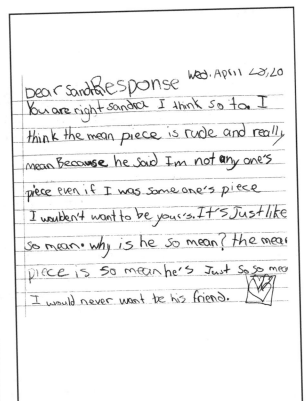

The Missing little piece

Dear Amber
The miss a piese he
went to find if he found
a piece, it was mean
becaues the piece said
"I'm not your piece if
I am I don't want to
be you peice". So he
went away he found
Another I think he was
Scare becaues last times
piece shout at him. but this
one dinit and they Fit
So he sing a song but he
can't sing sohe put the vice down
And he could sing I think that
was his mouth. I like the book becase
was his mouth. I like it was interesting.

Response Wed. April 28, 20
Dear Sandra
You are right sandra I think so to. I
think the mean piece is rude and really
mean Because he said I'm not any one's
piece even if I was some one's piece
I woulden't want to be yours. It's Just like
so mean. why is he so mean? the mean
piece is so mean he's Just so so mean
I would never want be his friend.

ILLUSTRATION 4.9 Using the dialogue journal, these two Grade 2 girls connect to specific parts of the text and to each other.

As they network their thinking, exchange and share responses, they further capitalize on the social aspects of reading. Remember, too, that they are responding to different books, so their background knowledge and excitement about these books grows as they share their journal responses.

Teachers of younger students (Grades 2 to 4) need to read and respond to all of their students' journal responses. Teachers of older students (Grades 5 and up) need not read every response but should read and respond to most. Sometimes students will request a focus for the teacher's responses: for example, "I don't understand why the character is acting this way. Do you?" or "I am trying to make better text-to-world connections. Please comment."

Carrie   Cleopatra, VII   Jan 31, 2000

Dear Melissa,
    Cleopatra is a great book. I feel so sorry for Cleopatra because she is stuck in Rome, where she doesn't have any friends in. And besides she is only twelve. She might look strong and brave outside, but they are not like that inside. That is what most authors do to their main characters. I guessed this one did that too. I don't think I want to live during the ancient times because you either be a slave or a worker, or part of the royal family or a general and lots more. Firstly I don't want to be a slave because it's unfair and there are a lot of work to do. I don't want to be a member of the royal family either because your brothers and sisters try to kill each other. Same with being a general. You can still get killed nowadays, but it's not as bad as it was like back then. Anyways, I think we should finish the book this week. Don't you? How do you like the book? What do you think of Cleopatra?
      Happy Responding & Reading,
      MELONHEAD

Yo, Carrier
    I agree that this book is great. I also feel sorry for Cleopat. that she doesn't ha a friend exept for h maid Neva. Neva is nice, I like Neva. I would like to be a member of the royal fami exept I would like to be the only child. I think that Cleopatra is very brave and kind.

Melissa

The Royal Diary.
Cleopatra VII

ILLUSTRATION 4.10 An amusing dialogue journal prepared by a pair of Grade 7 girls.

BUILDING AND USING CRITERIA FOR RESPONSE JOURNALS

When students are involved in building criteria for their response journals, they tend to write stronger responses. And we as teachers know that explicit expectations inspire stronger responses than implicit expectations The criteria-building process should take place over several days as a class. Teacher and students will examine various student responses, searching for what's powerful and use this to begin to build criteria. Try the following steps:

1. Listen to the responses and think about what worked, what was powerful. Write these on the overhead. If criteria-making is new to you, check out your provincial or state performance standards, which will help guide you toward grade-appropriate expectations for students. Use your performance standards only as a guide, not as a checklist, as more learning will occur when you build from the students' experiences and move toward the common goals of the standards.

2. Once you have shared four or five responses, examine the collected list and rearrange the list into several categories. These categories will become apparent as you examine the list.

3. For several days, have students practise writing responses according to these categories.

4. Refine the categories based on the feedback you have received from working with them and add several examples from student work to each category. This is now your criteria list; it has been developed from student experience and reflection on their own work and guided on the side by your performance standards.

Once you have successfully established the list of criteria, ensure that each student has a copy handy for when they are writing a response (see Illus. 4.4). Have students set goals for their writing according to the criteria list, and each week ask them to self-assess one of their responses. Read students' journals yourself and respond to them according to the criteria list.

Some teachers read and respond to each journal entry written by each student, some to only one entry per week per student. You will be able to determine how often you can and need to respond. Descriptive teacher responses best support learning. For example, you might say to Jake, the student who responded to *Terror in the Harbour* (Illus. 4.4), "I noticed that you felt sad like Penelope when she lost her dad. Have you ever had a time when you lost your dad? Were you searching for him as she was?" This will help Jake understand that what he did matched the criteria and scaffolds for him what to do next. Descriptive feedback is much more effective in promoting extended thinking than assigning a mark, which tends to terminate thinking. In fact, it is inappropriate to assign a mark or a letter grade at this time. Students

CRITERIA	WHAT IT LOOKS LIKE
Summarize the main idea	Just now, Charlie won the Golden Ticket. With the ticket he gets to visit Willie Wonka's Factory (Dahl, *Charlie and the Chocolate Factory*).
Key people/Key places	Spike is a very old dog. He is very grumpy. But when he sees Miss Darly he falls in love and is so happy (Baglio, *Pup at the Palace*). The places in this book are the inside of a peach, Aunt Sponge's house and beside the lake. I really liked how they traveled inside the peach on the way to New York (Dahl, *James and the Giant Peach*).
Ask questions	Why is the title *Liar, Liar, Pants on Fire*? How old is Zoe? Why does she tell so many lies? (Korman, *Liar, Liar, Pants on Fire*).
Make connections to self, text, world	Harold and I both have cats. His cat's name is Chester and mine is Gizzie. My cat died before I got my dogs. We have three dogs and he only has one (Howe and Howe, *Bunnicula*).

ILLUSTRATION 4.11 A criteria list developed by a Grade 3–4 class. This process took two weeks. This criteria list is pasted into each student's response journal.

need more practice with the criteria before any grades are assigned. They also need to experience the benefit of sharing their journal entries with other students informally (without using the list of criteria) and then more formally (using the criteria sheet for feedback).

At some point in your literature circles unit, you will need to gather marks. To support student learning and help students prepare for grades, first have them choose one sample response. This should occur after much descriptive feedback and many journaling opportunities. Evaluate and grade these samples, then return them to the students for more practice with the criteria list. When it is time for the grade that counts, either count this first grade and have students choose two more journal samples for grading or have students choose their three best responses. They should easily be able to make appropriate choices because the criteria are now so familiar to them. This becomes the journal mark.

EDITING IN ACTION

Normally, journal entries should not be edited or rewritten. Rather, it is more important to work at making the criteria explicit and spend time practising responses than it is to edit a journal entry after it has been committed.

On the other hand, older students can benefit from editing and rewriting by working with the list of criteria in an ongoing way. I present two different ways to do this: students choosing criteria and the class choosing the criteria.

Students Choosing Criteria

Having students choose the criteria for editing journal responses is a particularly effective method when students have had experience working with criteria. This is a process with a great deal of student choice. Try these steps:

1. Brainstorm with the class to come up with a list of criteria for powerful journal responses. From the brainstormed criteria list, each student chooses three criteria on which he or she wants to work. Have students list these criteria down the left-hand side of a chart and place the categories Good, Better, and Wow! across the top of the chart.

2. Each student chooses one journal response of his or her own to edit.

3. Students work in pairs, not necessarily with a partner who is reading the same book.

4. Each student reads his or her own journal response and finds evidence of the three criteria they have chosen.

5. The evidence is written in the Good column.

6. Students meet in pairs and share their journal responses and their evidence.

7. Together, students rewrite the Good example to make it Better.

	GOOD	BETTER	WOW!
1) emotion	I felt happy.	I felt happy when the dog licked her face.	I smiled to myself when the dog licked her face.
2) personal reaction	I didn't like it.	I didn't like the ending.	I didn't like the ending beacuse it left me with questions.
3) made connections in the story	This happened to me.	When I was skateboarding I fell too.	When I was skateboarding I didn't need a cast, just an elastic bandage.

ILLUSTRATION 4.12 An example of a Grade 7 student's personal criteria sheet for editing journal responses.

8. The student pair meets with the teacher to share their Better response, and the teacher, if possible, suggests ways to make it into a Wow! response.

9. Student pairs rewrite the examples to make them Wow! responses.

10. Each student rewrites his or her journal entry, incorporating the Wow! response.

The Class Choosing the Criteria

Having the class choose the criteria for editing responses is effective when the class is new to you or is less experienced working with criteria. You as teacher have more control than when students choose the criteria. Some teachers prefer this option because it allows them to make more exact connections with stated curriculum expectations. Try these steps:

1. As a class, determine three criteria on which to focus. Write these on the left-hand side of a chart.

2. Across the top of the chart, make columns entitled Good Start, Even Better, and Wow!

CRITERIA			
	GOOD START	**EVEN BETTER**	**WOW!**
Everybody Loves Details • details to paint a picture • use specific examples	Willow looks after her brother.	Willow holds his hand even when Twig does not want to.	Willow is loyal by holding Twig's hand, even when he resists.
Recipe for Reflection • goals, predictions summary, quotations • character, plot or setting development	I predict that Gram will take care of them.	I predict that Gram will be surprised to see them but she will take care of them.	I predict that Gram will be surprised that they could find her when they were alone and that she will welcome them.
The Big Picture • personal connections, comparisons, issues or themes	Lots of kids help with with their younger brothers.	Lots of kids help with their younger brothers, but Twig is very special.	I don't know if I could be as responsible as Willow and be mom and sister to Twig.

ILLUSTRATION 4.13 The teacher and the Grade 6-7 class together have agreed upon a set of criteria. Students identify examples of the criteria in their own work and place them in the Good Start category.

3. Each student chooses one journal response to edit from his or her own work.

4. Students work in pairs, and the partner need not necessarily be a student who is reading the same book.

5. Each student reads his or her own journal response, finds examples of the three criteria, and places a note about the examples in the Good Start column.

6. Students meet in pairs and share their journal response and their examples.

7. Together, students rewrite the Good Start example so that it can be placed in the Even Better column.

8. The student pairs meet with the teacher to share their Even Better responses, and the teacher suggests ways to make them into Wow! responses.

9. Student pairs rewrite the examples to make them Wow!

10. Students rewrite their journal entries.

COMPREHENSION ACTIVITIES

It is important to make comprehension the focus of literature circles regularly, and I believe every two weeks is an effective schedule. The students have already been reading and responding, analyzing, connecting, and offering opinions and reactions in group discussions and in their journals. Now, with a focus on comprehension, they begin to work with aspects of story structures, such as setting, character, and plot. They also may examine relationships among ideas and interpret themes. The particular comprehension activity you choose is determined by the needs of the students and the expectations of their particular curriculum. Since the students are already involved in frequent writing activities in their journal responses, comprehension activities are designed to develop comprehension in other ways: students work beyond the linguistic and intrapersonal intelligences that they practise in their journals. The variety of comprehension strategies you choose requires thinking with interpersonal, kinesthetic, visual-spatial, and/or logical-mathematical intelligence. Comprehension activities should be undertaken at the class level rather than within the literature circles and should not be started for two weeks, by which time most students will have read one book. Ideally, each comprehension activity should be completed in sixty to eighty minutes of class time.

HOW TO TEACH COMPREHENSION ACTIVITIES

Because the first comprehension activity is not introduced until the end of the second week of literature circles, most students will have finished at least one novel. It is important that students choose a novel that they have completed, or have almost completed, for their comprehension activity. All students will be working with the same comprehension activity, but students will be working on different novels. A student might use the same novel for two different comprehension activities—for example, if she or he takes four weeks to read one novel—but this is rare. In fact, students learn more effectively if they are able to work with a different novel for each comprehension activity. Try these steps:

1. Explain the purpose of the particular comprehension activity.

2. Model the comprehension activity with the class, using a text that everyone has read, perhaps a whole-class novel that was studied earlier in the year, before literature circles begin.

3. Decide with the students how the product (what they produce out of the comprehension activity) will be judged.

4. Build a new set of criteria or adapt criteria from a previous assignment. (This process becomes very quick and fluid as the students gain experience with it.)

5. As the students work on their assignments, move about the class, talking with them individually and in small groups, encouraging collaboration and providing support as needed.

KINDS OF COMPREHENSION ACTIVITES

Working with the Setting

Purpose: To have students use both visual and verbal thinking to consider the setting of their novel and how the setting affects the plot. Have students:

1. set up a page as a T-chart, with space above the top of the T; add two horizontal lines across the the perpendicular line of the T, creating six boxes;

2. answer the questions Where? and When? as they describe in detail (at the top of the chart) the general setting of the novel;

3. try to imagine themselves as roving photographers, moving through the landscape of the novel and changing lenses from a wide-angle lens for faraway shots to a telescopic lens for a close-up;

4. choose three particular scenes or settings and draw each setting; on the right-hand side, students write an explaination of what is

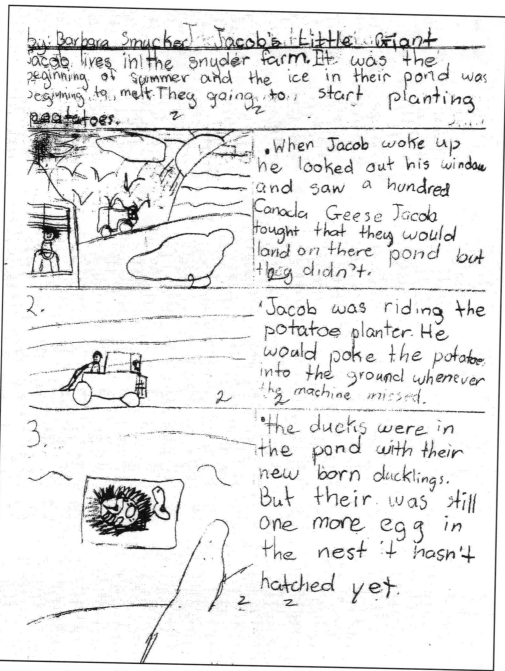

by: Barbara Smucker Jacob's Little Giant

Jacob lives in the snuder farm. It was the beginning of summer and the ice in their pond was beginning to melt. They going to start planting paatatoes.

.When Jacob woke up he looked out his window and saw a hundred Canada Geese Jacob tought that they would land on there pond but they didn't.

2.

'Jacob was riding the potatoe planter. He would poke the potatoe into the ground whenever the machine missed.

3.

'The ducks were in the pond with their new born ducklings. But their was still one more egg in the nest it hasn't hatched yet.

ILLUSTRATION 5.1 Regine, a Grade 4 student, has identified the general setting of Jacob's Little Giant (Smucker) and has drawn three specific images.

ILLUSTRATION 5.2 Jordan creates his character chart.

happening in the setting or (depending on the age and skill of the students) its significance.

Marking:

2 marks for each of the two questions related to the general setting (where and when) described at the top of the chart (4)

2 marks for each image drawn (on the left-hand side of the T) (6)

2 marks for each image described (on the right-hand side of the T) (6)

Total: 16 marks

Work with the students to develop examples of the quality of work that would be required for 2 marks. Play with 1-mark examples and show how to turn them into 2-mark examples.

Making Character Charts

Purpose: To undertake an in-depth study of a main character in a novel and his or her characteristics. Students will learn to describe characteristics and find supporting evidence for these characteristics by what the characters do, what the characters say, and what other characters say about them. Have students try these steps:

1. Set up a page as a T-chart.

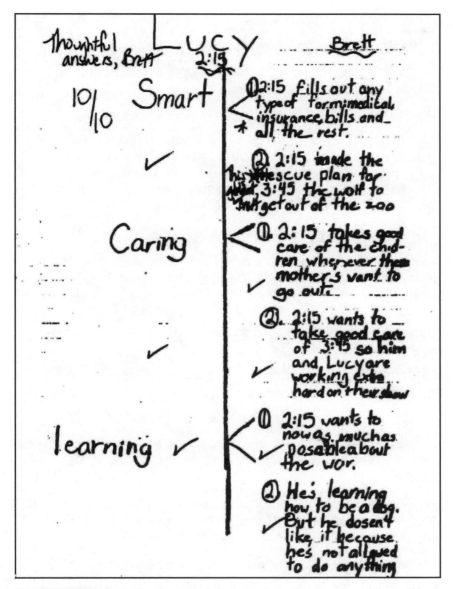

thoughtful answers, Brett

LUCY 2:15

Brett

10/10 Smart

✓

① 2:15 fills out any type of form; medical, insurance, bills and all the rest. *

② 2:15 made the rescue plan for 3:45 the wolf to get out of the zoo

Caring

✓

① 2:15 takes good care of the children whenever their mother's want to go out.

② 2:15 wants to take good care of 3:45 so him and Lucy are working extra hard on their show

learning ✓

① 2:15 wants to now as much as posable about the wor.

② He's learning how to be a dog. But he dosen't like it because hes not allowed to do anything

ILLUSTRATION 5.3 Brett, a Grade 5 student, analyzes the character of the wolf in the novel Lucy Keeps the Wolf from the Door (Jungman).

2. Choose a character.

3. Choose three key characteristics of the character.

4. Find two pieces of evidence in the text to support each of the three characteristics.

Marking:

  2 marks for each of three characteristics (6)

  2 marks for finding each of two pieces of supporting evidence in the text for each of the three characteristics (12)

  Total: 18 marks

Younger students are often challenged to find words to describe personality characteristics and tend to describe physical characteristics instead. A good way to help students understand the difference is to sketch a body shape and write the physical descriptions outside the body and the personality descriptions inside the head.

Speaking in Role: "Talk Show" Hot Seat

Purpose: To help students develop a deeper understanding of the characters in the novel. As they work together to simulate a talk show that includes several of the main characters from a novel they have all read, students will analyze the relationships among the characters and come to understand their actions and gain insights into their thinking. Try these steps:

1. Arrange students in teams, each team representing a novel that all students on the team have read.

2. Have students identify the main characters in the novel and who will represente each.

3. Invite students, as a team, in-role, to be interviewed in a "talk-show" setting.

4. To prepare for the interview, students explore questions that could be asked of each character and how these questions could be answered.

5. Begin the "talk show." All members of the team representing the novel appear together, all in-role. Assign the role of host to one of the students or take it on yourself. The remainder of the students take on the role of audience. The host provides a brief background. The students in the audience pose questions to the student in the "hot seat."

6. After allowing five or ten minutes of questioning one team, place a new team on the "hot seat."

Marking: Rather than marking students on their work in-role, have them write a reflection of the "talk show," describing how being in-role helped their understanding of the novel, how they stayed in-role, or how they felt their performance worked.

Making a Venn Diagram

Purpose: To use a Venn diagram to recognize similarities and differences beween two different aspects of a novel. A Venn diagram could be used, for example, to analyze the similarities and differences between two different novels, between a novel and a film based on the novel, or between students' lives and the lives of characters in the novel. I present two examples here: the first with students in a Grade 4-5 class, the second with students in Grade 7.

Marking for the Grade 4-5 Class Example:

In the Grade 4-5 class example, I asked the students to compare several aspects of their lives with those of the characters in historical novels, for example: homes, cities towns, or other geographic areas; daily chores; personal challenges.

1 mark for each of three pieces of evidence for each Then and each Now (3), or two marks each for two well-developed pieces of evidence (4)

1 mark for one piece of evidence for Shared (4)

Total marks: 7 or 9 (depending on the number of pieces of evidence and their detail)

Marking for Grade 7 Class Example:

In the Grade 7 example, I asked students to combine a character chart and a Venn diagram for two characters in two different novels. This allows for an analysis of two characters across two novels.

1 mark for describing each of three characteristics for the two characters (6)

1 mark for each of the two shared characteristics in the middle circle of the Venn diagram (2)

1 mark for each piece of evidence to support each characteristic (12 from individuals and 4 for shared = 16)

Total marks: 24

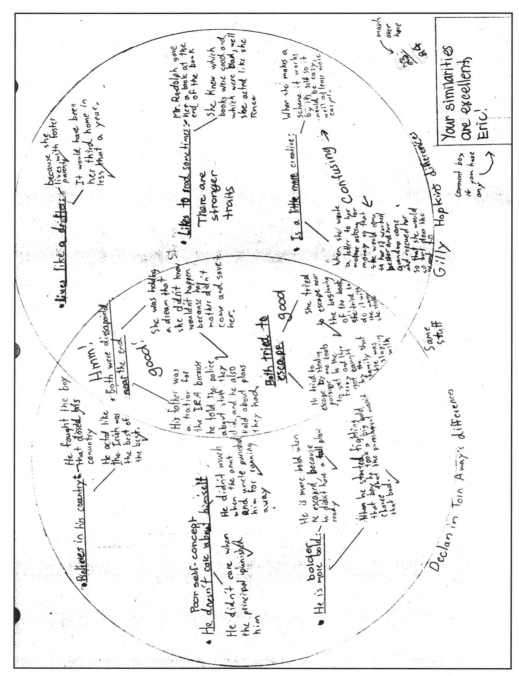

ILLUSTRATION 5.4 Eric, a Grade 7 student, compares Declan from Torn Away (Heneghan) and Gilly Hopkins from The Great Gilly Hopkins (Paterson).

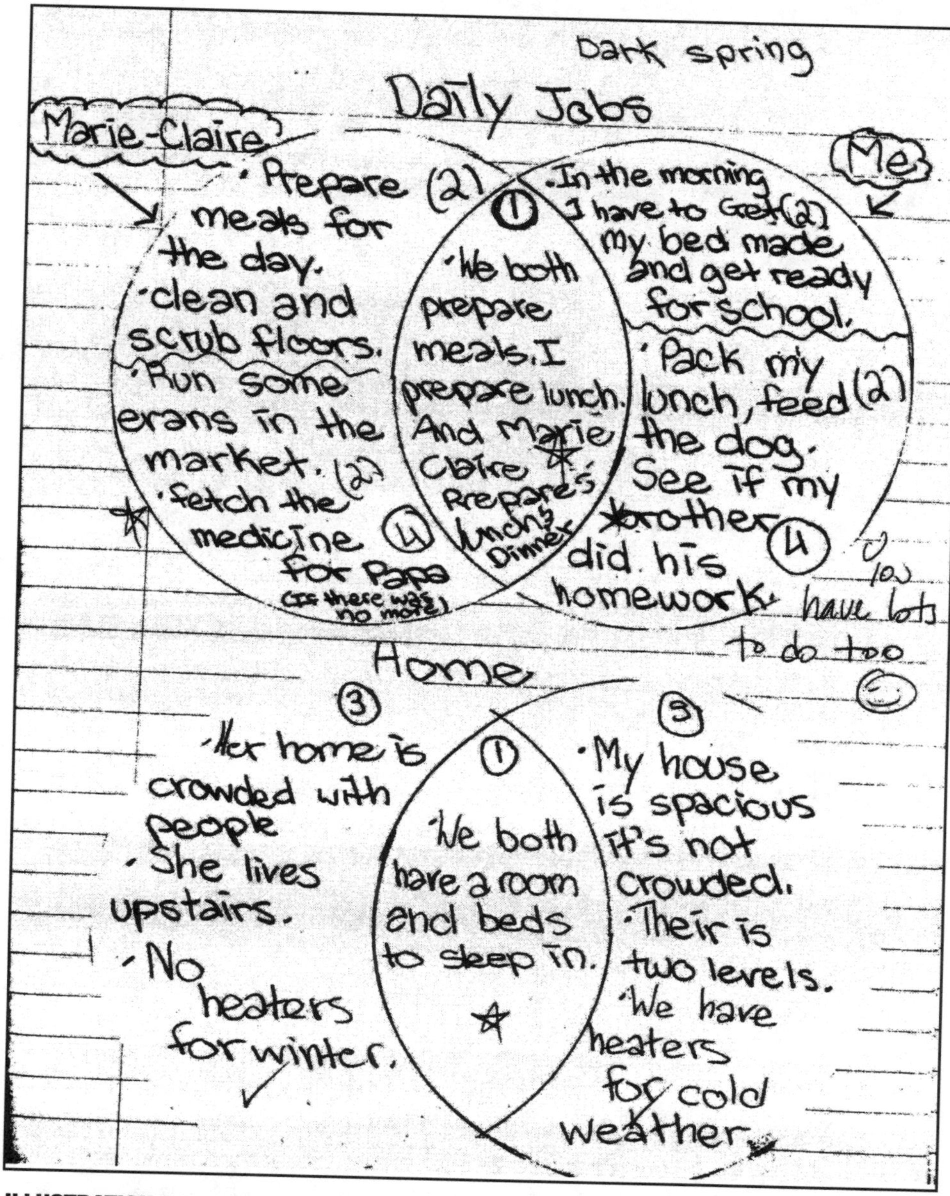

Dark spring

Daily Jobs

Marie-Claire

Me

- Prepare (2) meals for the day.
- clean and scrub floors.
- Run some erans in the market. (2)
- fetch the medicine for Papa (if there was no more)

① · We both prepare meals. I prepare lunch. And Marie Claire ✱ Prepares Lunch/Dinner ④

· In the morning I have to Get (2) my bed made and get ready for school.
· Pack my lunch, feed (2) the dog.
· See if my brother did his homework. ④

③ ④

have lots to do too

Home

③ · Her home is crowded with people
· She lives upstairs.
· No heaters for winter. ✓

① We both have a room and beds to sleep in. ✱

⑤ · My house is spacious It's not crowded.
· Their is two levels.
· We have heaters for cold weather.

ILLUSTRATION 5.5 In this Venn diagram developed by a Grade 4 student, the student has compared herself with Marie-Claire, the protagonist of Dark Spring (Stinson). The circled figures indicate highest possible marks, while the figures in parentheses indicate her personal scoring.

53

ILLUSTRATION 5.6 Colin (right) and Annan are reading Terror in the Harbour (McKay). Colin has created a submarine that includes images of a piece of glass, a clock, and three girls. Annan has created a house with a buggy, a deck from the boat where Penelope's father was working, and the two ships that collided.

Making Containers for Characters

Purpose: To help students gain a deeper understanding of the characters in a novel by working in a different medium (in this case producing a physical representation) that represent the characters. Have them work with plasticene or play dough to create a container for a character. As they work with this medium, they talk about the books they have chosen, the characters in the books, and the representations that they are creating. It is interesting to note how certain students excel when creating a physical representation and some are more comfortable creating a written representation. Try these steps:

1. Provide students with plasticene or play dough.

2. Ask each student to make a container that represents him- or herself; have each ask the questions Who am I? and What is important to me? This gives them a chance to practise a personal application of the strategy before applying the strategy to a character in their novel.

3. Have each student decorate the container with three symbols that further explain him- or herself; these should be details that enhance who the student is and what the student values.

ILLUSTRATION 5.7 An example of containers that a Grade 7 student has constructed to represent herself and her chosen character. Vivien has chosen a rainbow for herself (lower right) and a hen house (upper right), containing a basket, eggs, and a painting, to represent Julianna in Flipped (Van Draanen). She explains the connections for herself and for her chosen character. (The containers on the left are those of another student.)

VIVIEN

Rainbow - First word that comes to mind. Colorful. I have many different sides and so many ideas flowing in my mind all the time...I can't help it.

Ice cream – They say there's a pot of gold at the end of every rainbow and ice cream is my form of gold. I believe that every once in a while we should just let free and relax...indulge in something you truly love...

Bubbles – There's one word I would use to describe my personality...bubbly. All-round I'm a pretty optimistic and jolly person (sort of reminds you of Santa)...most of the time. But just like bubbles, they can pop anytime...and I tend to have a short-temper and little patience, just like the soapy substance.

Clothes – Color-coordination. I don't know what my life would be without it. In a way, it would reflect my creative side, down to every...single...last...detail. That's also another thing, I pay real close to attention to details. So close that it has become a part of me.

JULIANNA – FROM *FLIPPED*

Hen House – Even though their backyard is extremely dirty, still she goes out every day to feed and talk to the chickens. She didn't abandon them after she finished with her project; she kept them and raised them like they were her own children. Just that alone tells you what kind of person she is. It's a shame that there aren't more people like her nowadays.

Basket – Her thoughtfulness towards others really showed when she bided on the basket boy when no one else would. To further boost his confidence, she even got another person to help her increase the "going" price. Now that's something.

Eggs – Into the egg carton, across the street, in Bryce's hands, then chucked into the garbage. When she found that out...well, you could say that Bryce threw away a small part of a wonderful person with a big heart.

Painting – She's able to tell her father just about anything. And even if she doesn't, he can sense it. This stands for how strong their father/daughter relationship really is. To add to that, he even painted a picture of one of the things she loves most, her sycamore tree.

4. Discuss with students how they would like to be judged on their representations. I have found that most students feel that, since this is such a highly personal exercise, if they have completed a container that includes three symbols, they should receive full marks.

5. Broaden the discussion to include the importance of the audience being able to "read" the containers and the symbols.

6. Have students take a gallery walk about the room to examine the containers and symbols.

7. Give each student a new piece of plasticene or play dough or have them rework the first piece and have students make a container to represent a character from their chosen novel.

8. Ask students to decorate this container with three symbols in the same way that they did with their personal piece: details to enhance who the character is and what the character values.

9. Have students again take a gallery walk to examine the containers.

Marking:

2 marks for constructing the container (2)

3 marks for the addition of each of three symbols (9)

Total: 11 marks

Older students can be expected to find eight or ten phrases from the text to support their representation or interpretation of the character or to do a "quick write" to explain their choices. This is demonstrated in Vivien's work (Illus. 5.7).

Building a Readers' Theater

Purpose: To help students gain a deeper understanding of the plot and how it affects the lives of the characters by dramatizing extracts from a novel. Have students choose, write, and present to the class a particular scene from a novel. Have them practise writing dialogue for a dramatization, in which they will need to try changing the narrator's voice to the voice of characters. Try these steps:

1. Arrange students in teams in which all members have read the same novel, and have each team choose a scene to present.

READERS' THEATRE

Names_____ _____

Novel: _____

Scene: _____

Givens: • all students are included   • the climax of the novel is NOT presented

3 – accomplished   2 – satisfactory   1 – working on it

CRITERIA:	COMMENTS/MARK
• You kept within the time limit (3-5 minutes)	(only worth 1 mark)
• You chose a powerful or emotional scene	(all others – 3 possible marks)
• You maintained your concentration	
• You were well-organized and prepared, knowing your lines	
• We could see you and hear you	
• You went beyond expectations with something personal	
Total: 16	

ILLUSTRATION 5.8 The criteria sheet prepared by a Grade 6-7 class for their readers' theater presentations.

2. Have students use the existing dialogue contained in the chosen text as a starting point.

3. Ask students to rewrite the surrounding (narrative) text as dialogue, as it is needed.

4. Have students practise reading the dialogue.

5. Arrange for teams to present their Readers' Theater to the rest of the class.

Marking: For Readers' Theater, I have found that peer- and self-evaluation works well. In my experience team-teaching a Grade 6-7 class, as each team presented, we had groups of students (chosen randomly but including all students in one peer evaluation), complete a criteria form. After the students completed their Readers' Theater, they compiled the criteria form as a self-evaluation. Finally, we (teachers) evaluated each team.

Forming a Tableau

Purpose: To have students work together and use their bodies to understand a scene from a novel. Forming a tableau helps them create a mental picture of what is happening in the text and helps to raise their level of comprehension. Try these steps:

1. Arrange students in teams of four to seven students. Have each team pick a scene that they would like to present from a novel that they have all read.
2. Ask students to arrange their bodies to create the scene, then freeze in place.
3. Have each team present its scene to the rest of the class.
4. Ask a student from the class to tap each member of the tableau in turn; the tapped student explains who or what he or she represents in the scene.

Marking: Rather than assigning specific marks for each student or each team, I think self-evaluation works best for the Tableau. Have students reflect about:

- what they are most proud of in their performance;
- what they hoped the audience noticed about the performance;
- a goal for next time;
- what they learned from working with others.

Taking a Learning Journey

Purpose: To help students move beyond just the retelling of a story to respond to what happens to the lead character by describing key events as a journey. (In the novel, through a series of events, the character learns how to reach his goal; he has completed a learning

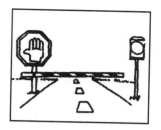 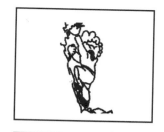 

ILLUSTRATION 5.9 Icons for learning journeys (Brownlie and King, Learning in Safe Schools, p. 43, illustrations by Riffe Bauman).

ILLUSTRATION 5.10 A Grade 8 student uses icons to present Joey's learning journey in War Horse (Morpurgo).

DESIGN: (POSSIBLE 1)
Bold
Colourful
Frame
Neat

LEARNING JOURNEY: (POSSIBLE 2)
Beginning, Middle, End
What s/he learned

DETAIL: (POSSIBLE 3)
3 details

ICONS: (POSSIBLE 1)
Used 6 icons

ILLUSTRATION 5.11 The criteria sheet prepared by a Grade 4-5 class for a learning journey.

journey.) Students use metaphor and incorporate such terms as *road-blocks, just rolling along, needing support from others.* Try these steps:

1. Display the icons for a learning journey (see Illus. 5.9) and discuss what each could mean. Invite students to invent other icons.

2. Discuss the learning journey of a character in a book that all students have read.

3. Match the icons to events in the characters' lives.

4. Have the class develop the criteria for a successful learning journey.

5. Have each student design the learning journey for his or her character, following the criteria.

Marking: Students self-evaluate using the criteria sheet then hand in their learning journey for teacher evaluation. Criteria should focus on the metaphor and the thinking, not just on presentation.

Having a Pair Discussion

Purpose: To allow students to discuss specific, open-ended questions with others before writing about their novels. The questions can be generated by the teacher or the students and are designed to frame the discussion, often leading students to connections and discoveries that they might not have had on their own, thus deepening their understanding. Try these steps:

1. Arrange students in pairs; both students will have finished reading the book.

2. Have students choose a question or two that they would like to discuss (or present one yourself).

3. Students spend five or ten minutes discussing one or two questions with their partners (discussion time increases as students become more skilled).

4. Have students change partners, choose new questions, and continue to discuss. This is a whole-class activity, but the discussing pairs have read the same book.

5. Have students try to respond to questions with specific examples from the text and with connections from their lives, other texts, and the wider world. Make this criterion explicit to all.

6. Have students write in their journals a response to one of the questions, following the set criteria.

Marking: Students self-evaluate their written responses, using the given criteria that they have been practising with in their paired discussions.

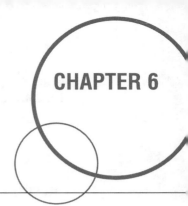

CHAPTER 6

CLASSROOM VIGNETTES

EXTRA SUPPORT FOR YOUNG READERS WRITING JOURNALS, GRADES 2 AND 3, WITH JENNIFER KATZ

Jennifer Katz found that all her Grade 2 and 3 students could begin working with a double-entry journal, whether they were reading independently or whether they were working within their guided reading groups. But because she thought they needed a little more support in retelling and in explaining their connections and questions, and with their responses, she designed a more structured response form for the first few sessions. As students learned to work with the more structured framework, she invited them to use the more open design: What Happened/My Thinking.

FROM SLAVERY TO FREEDOM: LOOKING AT NON-FICTION READING, GRADES 5 AND 6, WITH NICOLE WIDDESS

Nicole Widdess's dual goal was to teach non-fiction reading and explore slavery: an interdisciplinary endeavor. During the first week, she involved the whole class in read-aloud picture books, both fiction and non-fiction. She also taught specific reading and response strategies such as Four Quadrants (Brownlie, Feniak, McCarthy), Reading as a Writer (Brownlie, Close, Wingren), Writing in Role (Brownlie, Close, Wingren), Thinking Bubbles (Brownlie, Close, Wingren), Think Alouds (Harvey), and Three-Column Notes (Santa) to build background knowledge and to teach effective reading as thinking. She included these books:

Hopkinson, *Sweet Clara and the Freedom Quilt* [picture book, fiction]

Lester, *From Slave Ship to Freedom Road* [picture book, non-fiction]

Ringgold, *Aunt Harriet's Underground Railroad in the Sky* [picture book, fiction]

Winters, *Follow the Drinking Gourd* [picture book, fiction]

In the second and third weeks, Nicole focused on shared reading. She included these books:

*Kositsky, *Rachel: A Mighty Big Imagining* [fiction]

Greenwood, *The Last Safe House* [non-fiction]

By week four, Nicole's students were reading their own novels and moving into literature circle discussion groups. Her book list included:

Collier and Collier, *Jump Ship to Freedom*

Haskens, *Get on Board: The Story of the Underground Railroad* [non-fiction]

*Kositsky, *The Maybe House*

Lyons, *Letters from a Slave Girl* [challenging]

Paterson, *Jip: His Story*

Paulsen, *Sarny: A Life Remembered* [challenging]

In the weeks following week four, Nicole shifted the focus to transforming information gained into persuasive writing. Throughout the entire study, Nicole wove into the literature circles various other artistic media: water-color painting to develop holistic imagery; story-telling and mask-making to build text-to-text connections; examining a famous piece of art to introduce questioning; and quilting to develop symbols for important ideas.

WEAVING RESPONSE JOURNALS INTO LITERATURE CIRCLE DISCUSSION GROUPS, GRADES 6 AND 7, WITH KATHY PANTALEO

Kathy Pantaleo asked that her Grade 6 and 7 students come prepared with a passage to share and a response-in-progress to share. She instructed them to present their responses as letters to her. From time to time, the students reflected on their participation in their discussion group, using a Discussion Group Self-Evaluation Sheet (see Illus. 6.1).

Kathy gave her students the following instructions: After your discussion group session, please complete the self-evaluation sheet.

DISCUSSION-GROUP SELF-EVALUATION SHEET

After your discussion group, please complete the self-evaluation criteria list below. Next to each item, indicate by using 4 3 2 1 how you think you were. In the blank boxes below, tell me what you did well and where you could improve for next time. The content critera should also be used as a guide for your responses that are due on Friday.

PREPARATION • the givens are included (reading done, all materials ready, questions prepared) • detailed answers to question are prepared • list of general questions for discussion are prepared	
LISTENING • accepts what everyone says • uses good body language • makes eye contact • listens to speaker • uses encouraging sounds (mm mh, uh huh, I agree)	
PARTICIPATION • repsects other people's questions • lets people pass • takes turns • interrupts politely • continues on other people's ideas • tries to not read from his or her notes • provides input • asks questions of her or her peers • shows enthusiasm • encourages participation from others • asks a follow-up question	
CONTENT • support what you say with details and description • include a passage from the novel to support your ideas • make a connecction with yourself, another novel, or current events • include a voice in your writing; make sure it is well-written • describe the story elements (plot, theme, character development, setting	

ILLUSTRATION 6.1 Discussion Group Self-Evaluation Sheet.

Name HAYAMI

Reflections on the Slavery Unit

1. What did you enjoy about the slavery unit?

I enjoyed how I learned that life isn't always easy-peasy, that people had to work for someone every second of their day, and that their soul, their heart, their very breath belonged

2. What did you learn about slavery? someone you don't care about.

I learned that slaves were taken from their homes in Africa, and be forced to work for a master, and some slaves tried to escape to Canada to recieve what was

3. What else would you have liked to learn about slavery? rightfully theirs - free

I would have wanted to know why masters treated slaves with such disrespect, and if masters believed black people were just like them, that they had a soul and feeling

4. What new reading strategies have you learned?

I have learned to use the thought bubble, and it is my favorite strategy so far.

5. Which reading strategy did you like best? Why? Will you use it again?

I liked the thought bubble best, because I can include both pictures and words that come to my mind. I will use this strategy again, definately.

ILLUSTRATION 6.2 Grade 4 student Hayami reflects on his learning during the unit on slavery.

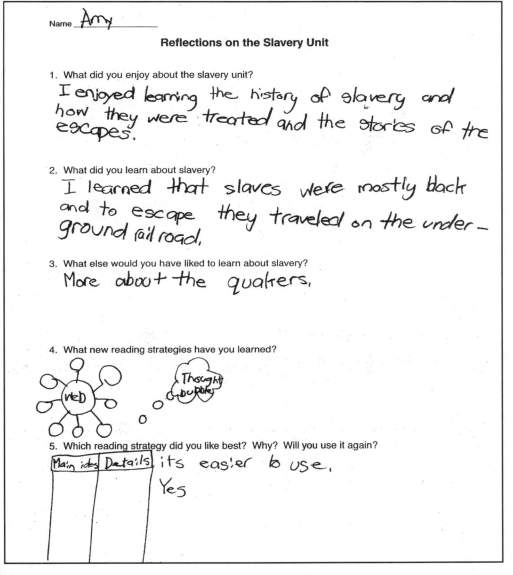

Name __Amy__

Reflections on the Slavery Unit

1. What did you enjoy about the slavery unit?

I enjoyed learning the history of slavery and how they were treated and the stories of the escapes.

2. What did you learn about slavery?

I learned that slaves were mostly black and to escape they traveled on the under-ground railroad.

3. What else would you have liked to learn about slavery?

More about the qualkers.

4. What new reading strategies have you learned?

web

Thought bubble

5. Which reading strategy did you like best? Why? Will you use it again?

| Main idea | Details | its easier to use. |

Yes

ILLUSTRATION 6.3 Grade 4 student Amy reflects on her learning during the unit on slavery. (Hayami [Illus. 6.2] talks about the power of combining visual and verbal thinking, but Amy demonstrates it.)

Next to each item, indicate with a 4, 3, 2, or 1 how you think you were. In the blank boxes, tell me what you did well and where you could improve for next time. Use the content criteria as a guide for your responses.

Kathy used a process similar to Editing in Action to help students write more sophisticated responses. She expected all students to focus

WHAT HAPPENED

Book Title: _____ Date: _____

In the beginning _____(character's name) was

(setting) _____

Two important events:

First,_____

_____

Then, _____

_____

In the end, _____

_____

_____

WHAT I THINK

Book Title: _____ Date: _____

I was thinking about _____

because _____

_____

I was wondering about_____

because _____

I was imagining _____

because _____

_____

I was feeling _____

_____

ILLUSTRATION 6.4 Sample of a BlackLine Master for young students who are just beginning to write double-entry journals.

RESPONSE JOURNAL EVALUATION SHEET

Name: _____

Title of Book: _____

Pages Read: _____ Date: _____

Please indicate below your evaluation of your response. The ideas listed below are to be used as a guideline, so do not feel that everything needs to be included in your response to have a strong mark. I am looking for a thoughtful, detailed response. Remember to write your response in the form of a letter to me!

Step 1: circle below your mark in the **Overall Picture** and **Summary** categories and include an example in the space provided.

Step 2: circle your mark below in **at least one** of the **Connection, Question** and **Big Ideas** categories. Also, include an example in the space provided.

Overall Picture   5 4 3 2 1
• includes details that make the response descriptive
• includes specific examples to support your ideas
  (remember that if you are including a passage from
  the novel to include quotations and the page number)
• includes new ideas and interest in the novel
• has good writing conventions (spelling, punctuation, etc.)

Summary   5 4 3 2 1
• clearly explains what happens
• includes the important events, and keeps to the storyline
• can include a prediction
• should be 4-5 sentences

Connection   5 4 3 2 1
• with your life, another novel, or an event in the world
• can use sentence starters such as "That reminds me of a time when..."

Question
• what you wonder about the author
• your thoughts about the character, setting, or events
• can include a prediction

Big Ideas
• how the character has changed
• interesting language
• the theme or moral
• thoughts and feelings about the novel
• recommendation or rating

ILLUSTRATION 6.5 A Response Journal Evaluation Sheet.

COURAGE – HOPE – POWER OF FAMILY – PERSECUTION – SURVIVAL

Over the next few weeks you will participate in literature circles, reading and discussing several books based on the themes shown above. Your main project is to create an "Ideagram".
There will be several progress checks before the due date, which will be at the end of our study.

What is an Ideagram?

An Ideagram is a visual display that represents a theme. It is a creative collection of quotes, personal responses, pictures, and drawings. It may look similar to the examples below.

How do I start?

• Collect evidence from as many themes as possible from your first 2 books before you decide on a definite theme. Select from: Courage, Survival, Power of Family, Persecution, Hope.

• Over the next few weeks, you need to look for evidence of your theme from a variety of resources in addition to your novel. Collect quotes and pictures from different sources (your novels, newspapers, magazines, song lyrics, poetry...)

• You will be provided with a graphic organizer to collect your quotes. You will have to organize your picture collection yourself.

Criteria:

1. You have a variety of visual representations.
2. You have included quotations from several of your books and included the page number and title.
3. Your display demonstrates "voice." You show your personal opinions or reflections on the theme.
4. You have shown connections to "outside sources" (news, magazines, poetry, song lyrics...) and cited the source.
5. Your display shows an emotional connection to the theme.
6. The audience will feel emotion when they view it.

_____

_____

Parents please sign to indicate your child has explained his/her responsibilities to you.

ILLUSTRATION 6.6 A contract explaining the expectations for an ideagram assignment and how it will be marked.

first on just two elements: (1) the overall picture and a summary and (2) to choose connections, questions, or big ideas. Each student chose a response, then they worked collaboratively on refining this response. After repeated practice on several responses, doing mini-lessons on areas of need, and much sharing, the students developed their evaluation sheet. Students chose a specific response for evaluation. They edited and polished as necessary, self-evaluated, and then handed in their responses to Kathy for final marking.

A CULMINATING ACTIVITY THAT BEGINS AT THE BEGINNING, GRADES 6 AND 7, WITH TINA PALI

Tina Pali, in planning a literature-circles unit on the themes of hope, power of family, persecution, and survival, wanted to use a culminating activity to help students synthesize their learning; she chose an ideagram. She introduced the concept of the ideagram to her students at the beginning of the unit so they could work with this end in mind and consult at checkpoints along the way. She developed a contract to clearly explain to the students and their parents her expectations (see Illus. 6.6).

Illustrations 6.7 and 6.8 show the high quality of work of the students in Tina's class. Courtney has added to her ideagram a series of letters that she has written, entitled "From the Diaries of Jews and Germans." She writes reflections of World War II from several different points of view: a Nazi soldier; a Jewish prisoner; a German who is anti-war. Charles has created a legend to aid the reader in understanding his diagram and connects explicitly the issue of slavery to that of the persecution of the Jews.

THE FINAL YEAR AND GOVERNMENT EXAMS, LITERATURE 12, WITH KRISTA EDIGER

Krista Ediger has been working with her Literature 12 students in literature circles. This is a course that culminates in an external government examination, preparation for which often directs the entire course. By using an eight-class time frame, she found that she was able to both cover the curriculum demands and allow choice for the students. She combined literature circles with a thematic unit on two topics—politics and power, and morality and ethics—in which she involved the students in discussion and in writing assignments, culminating with a major presentation. The novels she chose were:

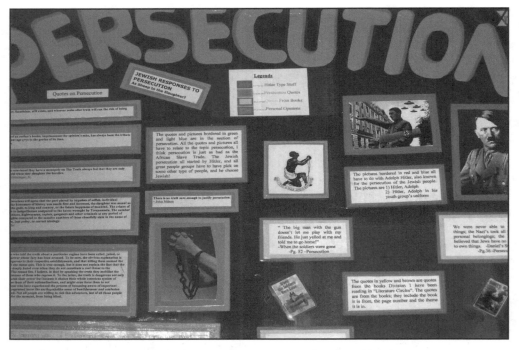

ILLUSTRATION 6.7 Ideagram produced by Grade 7 student Charles, which links persecution of slavery with that of the Jewish people during World War II.

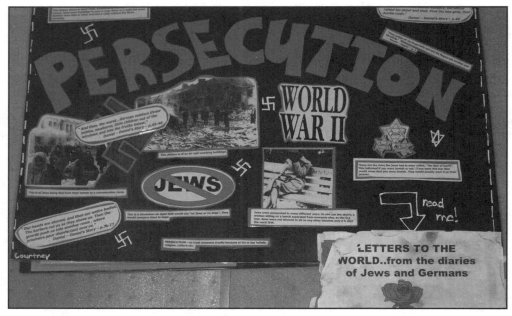

ILLUSTRATION 6.8 Ideagram produced by Grade 7 student Courtney, which focuses on the persecution of the Jews during World War II.

RATING	CRITERIA
Outstanding	Insightful and thorough. Criteria are clearly evident and discussed with supporting evidence.
Good	Complete and logical. Criteria are evident, are discussed with supporting evidence, but may be vague or missing in some places.
Satisfactory	Appropriate. Criteria are generally met, with some supporting evidence, although the support may be quite general or unclear.
Marginal	Limited analysis. Only partial criteria are in evidence. May be illogical.
Not Demonstrated	Incomplete, inappropriate, unsupported, illogical.

ILLUSTRATION 6.9 Quality of Self-Evaluation and Analysis Rating Scale used by Literature 12 students (British Columbia Ministry of Education, Enhancing and Evaluating Oral Communication in the Secondary Grades, p. 9:21).

Atwood, *The Handmaid's Tale*

Huxley, *Brave New World*

Orwell, *Nineteen Eighty-Four*

Krista encouraged her students to work in literature circles, but a few opted to work on their own. All were expected to read the allotted eighth (eight classes, one-eighth of the book per class) in order to be able to participate fully in the day's conversation. When it came time for evaluation, students who were in the discussion group did self-evaluations, and those who were working on their own used a quote-record journal format in which they essentially recorded only their own thinking. Krista then marked the students either on their group-discussion self-evaluations or on their personal journals. The self-evaluations were based on the following criteria:

- The student offers insightful interpretation with some depth of response and analysis (evidence of rereading and reflecting).

- The student shows commitment, pride, and satisfaction in his or her work.

- The student demonstrates a willingness to be open-minded and to show respect for textual evidence when sharing interpretations of literature.

- The student demonstrates an ability to not just listen to others' interpretations but also to consider others' ideas and integrate them into their own responses whenever possible.

The criteria for self-evaluation were scaled according to the Quality of Self-Evaluation and Analysis Rating Scale, adapted from the provincial curriculum (see Illus. 6.9).

Krista found that many students read at least two novels and moved among several discussion groups. "I saw," says Krista, "the same energy here in Grade 12 that everyone raves about with younger kids."

A CULMINATING ACTIVITY
TIME FOR CELEBRATION

Most teachers run their literature circles for six to eight weeks, though some teachers work with them for only three and a half weeks and some for most of the term. Whatever might be the amount of time a teacher chooses to spend at literature circles, as the end draws near, it is important to make preparations to celebrate all the reading the students have done. The period of time when students work within literature circles is usually the time of the year when they read the most, engage in more conversations about literature, and are most passionate about their reading. Try these ideas for celebrations:

1. Students work in teams of three, decide on their favorite books, and create a poster to advertise the books to other potential readers.

2. The class votes on which book read during literature circles was their favorite.

3. The class invites another class in to talk about their books. Students meet in twos and threes and talk about what they have read.

4. Students reflect on the question What has this book taught you about life and living? after they have read each book. Keeping this question in mind during their reading of a book helps them respond effectively when response time eventually comes.

As the time approaches to change to the celebration activity in your language arts, English or humanities classroom, announce the date that it will occur. This allows students to estimate how long they have left to finish their final book. Some teachers choose one of the comprehension activities as a final, celebratory activity. Popular choices are Containers for Characters and Talk Show Hot Seat. Allowing time

ILLUSTRATION 7.1 Ben and Gaby delight in sharing their reading.

and space for a specific culminating activity provides a sense of closure.

My final act of closure is always letter writing. I have the students write me a letter that reflects on their experience with literature circles and gives me advice for next time. There is no better way to refine your practice than by considering the effect of your decisions on the lives of the students. I have found these letters at various times to be powerful, thoughtful, humbling, and enlightening. I include here two examples. Colin is a Grade 5 student who had previously expended a lot of energy avoiding reading. Mika is a Grade 7 student who loves reading and spends a lot of time at it. These examples show how Colin's and Mika's experiences in literature circles have both touched their hearts and enhanced their senses of themselves as readers.

Thurs. May 6

Dear Mrs. Brownlie,

I really enjoy reading these books. My favorite book is Terror In The Harbour. I liked it because it has lots of deep feelings. I was shocked when I read that Penny had to stay home everyday and help around the house. Penny must be sad to have no mom.

For a next time, they should have a book that has less sad feelings and more happy feelings. They should have a book thats in the 1800s.

You might like to read Emily Carr's Woo.

MsB

Yours truly,
Colin

ILLUSTRATION 7.2 Notice how Colin's letter of advice to his teacher about his experiences in literature circles makes explicit connections to the text.

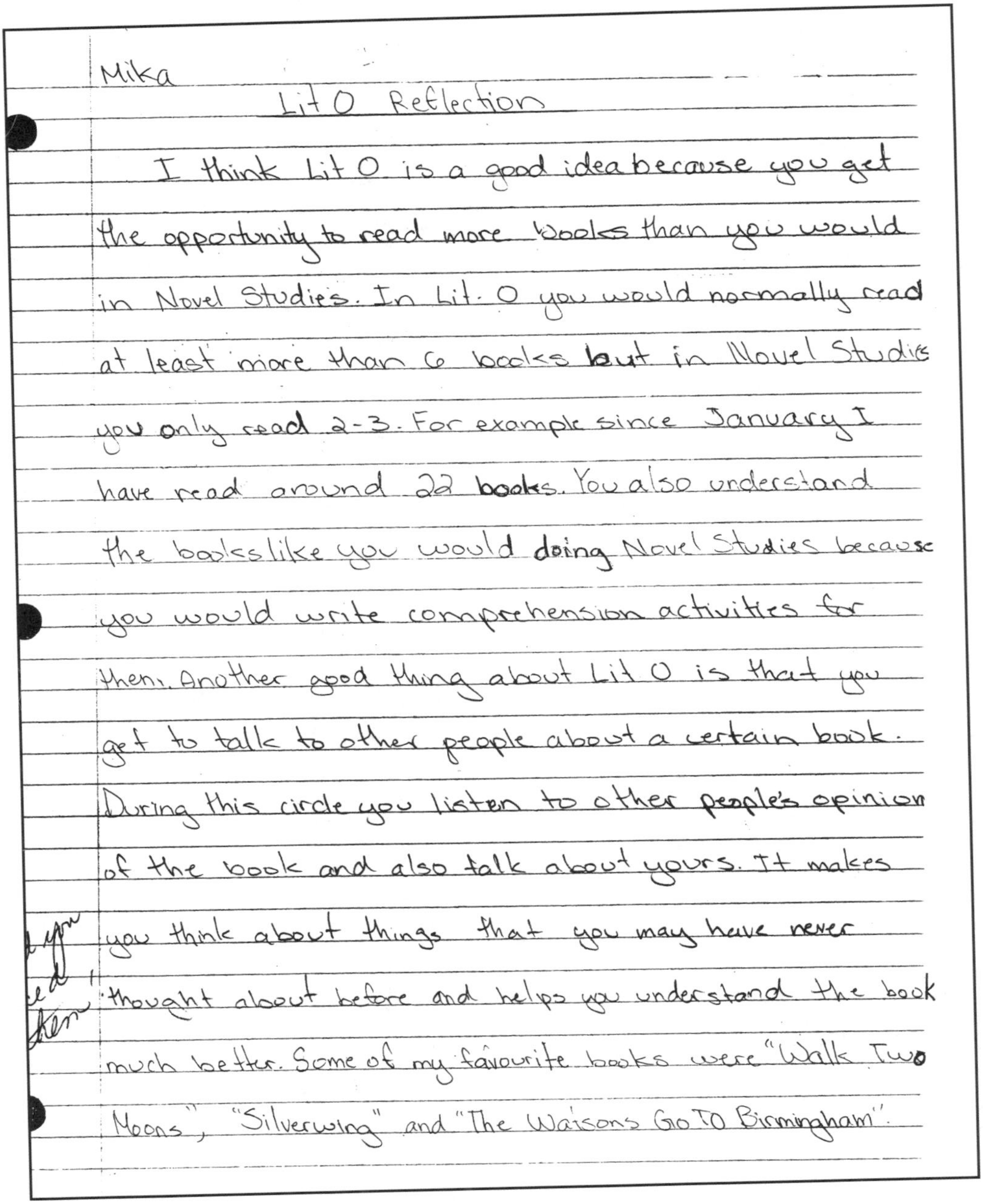

Mika

Lit 0 Reflection

I think Lit 0 is a good idea because you get the opportunity to read more books than you would in Novel Studies. In Lit. 0 you would normally read at least more than 6 books but in Novel Studies you only read 2-3. For example since January I have read around 22 books. You also understand the books like you would doing Novel Studies because you would write comprehension activities for them. Another good thing about Lit 0 is that you get to talk to other people about a certain book. During this circle you listen to other people's opinion of the book and also talk about yours. It makes you think about things that you may have never thought about before and helps you understand the book much better. Some of my favourite books were "Walk Two Moons", "Silverwing" and "The Watsons Go To Birmingham".

ILLUSTRATION 7.3 Notice in this excerpt from Mika's letter about her experiences in literature circles shows not only how many books she has read but also the effect that the conversations have had on her thinking.

CHAPTER 8

ASSESSMENT AND EVALUATION

A ssessment is descriptive information about learning. Assessment informs learners about how they are doing and helps them make plans and set goals for what to do next. During the time they have spent in literature circles, students have had many assessment opportunities. In collaboration with their teachers, they have built the criteria for responding and used these criteria both to guide their writing and thinking and to set personal goals. From their teachers' modeling, they are aware of and have discussed the behavior expected of them during literature-circles conversations. They have received descriptive feedback from their teachers, and sometimes from their peers, about their journals and their participation in the conversations. They have been advised of the minimum number of books that they need to read in the allotted time and encouraged to go beyond the minimum. They have been supported in making wise book choices: books that they can read and want to read. These ongoing assessment conversations (about what needs to be done and how they are doing with what needs to be done) serve to improve student learning for two reasons: they make the implicit explicit; they teach students to work with an end in mind.

Over several weeks, having received much feedback and worked with this in mind, the focus will begin to shift from assessment to evaluation. Evaluation is the measurement of learning. It is at this point that judgments about the accomplishments of learning are made.

Evaluation (the final grade) is a compilation of judgments about learning accomplishments from several aspects of literature circles. These include response-journal writing, literature-circles discussions, comprehension activities, number of books read, a personal interview or conference with the teachers, and, perhaps, a final culminating project. I discuss each of these here.

JOURNAL RESPONSES

1. After a set of criteria has been developed for journal responses (see Ch. 4) and the students have practised with the criteria and received descriptive feedback from the teacher (ideally once a week), have students submit one journal response for marking.

2. Respond to this journal with a mark and advice for improvement. This becomes one of the "exemplary journal responses."

3. Have students continue writing journal responses and choose two more journal responses for marking.

4. These three "exemplary journal responses" form the response journal mark.

LITERATURE CIRCLES DISCUSSIONS

1. Establish guidelines for appropriate behavior in the discussion groups (see Ch. 3).

2. Keep an anecdotal record of your observations of student behavior in the discussion groups.

3. Have students reflect on their behavior in the discussion group, using the guidelines.

4. Use these data to form the discussion group mark.

COMPREHENSION ACTIVITIES

1. Make a list of comprehension activities that can be used as a basis for scoring. Some teachers choose to include all of the comprehension activities the students have completed to date, while some teachers choose about three-quarters of them. Whichever you choose, the students will have co-created the criteria for each comprehension assignment (see Ch. 5).

2. Use this data to form the comprehension activities mark.

NUMBER OF BOOKS READ

Establish expectations for the minimum number of books that need to be read for an A grade, a B grade, or a C grade. You may need to adjust this minimum number based on the variation in length and complexity of some of the books.

CULMINATING PROJECT

1. If you choose to include a final project, develop criteria to guide the project with the students (see Ch. 6)

2. Use these criteria to form the basis for the mark.

INTERVIEW OR CONFERENCE

1. Some time during the course of the literature-circles unit, plan to have a personal interview with each student.

2. For the sample interview presented here (Illus. 8.1), I used as a guide the format developed by Sharon Jeroski, director of Horizon Research and head of the development team for *B.C. Performance Standards for Reading.*

3. Students come to the interview with a book that they have chosen.

4. The interview should take about five minutes per student.

5. Work with the question guide in hand and ask the student some of the questions.

6. Write the student's responses in the appropriate spaces on the Performance Standards Worksheet (see Illus. 8.2).

7. Notice that the strength of this format lies in the specific targeting toward the criteria that are described for the grade-appropriate performance standard and therefore does not allow the interview to roam at will. The conversation during this kind of interview makes direct links to the reader's strategies, comprehension, response and analysis.

8. Analyze the student responses against the Fully Meets Expectations descriptions and assign an appropriate mark.

CATEGORY	FULLY MEETS EXPECTATIONS	POSSIBLE CONFERENCE QUESTIONS/PROMPTS
STRATEGIES • check understanding • word skills • knowledge of genres • figurative language	• checks for understanding; adjusts strategies • uses a variety of strategies for new words • uses knowledge of familiar genres to predict or confirm meaning • recognizes and tries to interpret figurative language	• Was this story easy or hard for you to read? What makes it that way? • Are there any words that were hard for you at first? How did you figure them out? • What different strategies do you use to figure out unknown words? • Have you read other books in this genre? How are they like or unlike this one? • Can you give me an example of how knowing about this genre helps you predict or confirm meaning in this story? • Can you give me an example of figurative language in this story? Can you explain what that phrase/word/sentence means?
COMPREHENSION • story elements • predictions • inferences • details • theme	• describes story elements in own words; explains some relationships • makes logical predictions and inferences; when asked, can provide specific evidence • identifies relevant details in responses • interprets obvious themes	• Can you tell the plot so far? • Could this story have happened in a different setting? Why or why not? • Tell me about two different characters and explain their relationship. • What do you think will happen next? Why do you think so? • Can you describe the theme or the big idea behind this story? • Tell me, in some detail, about a piece of the story that really interests you.
RESPONSE AND ANALYSIS • connections to experiences and other selections • reactions	• makes and supports logical connections to self or other selections • offers reactions and opinions with some support	• Do any of the characters react in a way similar to you? Tell me about that. • Do you relate to or identify with any particular character or event in this story? Explain the relationship. • Are you liking this story? Why or why not? • To whom would you recommend this book? Why? • Is this a predictable text? • Is this text well-written? Why or why not? • Have you found lines or phrases in this book that you will use in your writing? Can you give an example? • Is this a compelling read? Why or why not?

ILLUSTRATION 8.1 A sample end-of-year interview for a Grade 7 student, based on the Fully Meets Expectations column of the Quick Scale of the B.C. Performance Standards for Reading Literature (British Columbia Ministry of Education). The questions I have generated are designed to elicit response targeted to the specific bullets on the performance standard.

SNAPSHOT	The student is able to read generally straightforward fiction and poetry and complete assigned tasks. Work is accurate and complete. Selection:_____	
ASPECT	**FULLY MEETS EXPECTATIONS (MAR-APR)**	
STRATEGIES • check understanding • word skills • knowledge of genres • figurative language	• checks for understanding; adjusts strategies • uses a variety of strategies for new words • uses knowledge of familiar genres to predict or confirm meaning • recognizes and tries to interpret figurative language	
COMPREHENSION • story elements • predictions • inferences • details • theme	• describes story elements in own words; explains some relationships • makes logical predictions and inferences; when asked, can provide specific evidence • describes story elements in own words; explains some relationships • makes logical predictions and inferences; when asked, can provide specific evidence • identifies relevant details in responses • interprets obvious themes	
RESPONSE AND ANALYSIS • connections to experiences • reactions	• makes and supports logical connections to self • offers reactions and opinions with some support	

ILLUSTRATION 8.2 Performance Standards Worksheet for recording a Grade 7 student's responses during the reading interview.

The collection and reporting of marks signals to students and parents some of the achievements made. This multi-faceted way of gathering data for a mark is fair to all students and honors both the reader and the reading. The marks reflect the measurement of learning that has occurred as a result of ongoing assessment conversations.

Teachers often report that their marks in literature circles are higher than marks in other aspects of their ELA program. This, I believe, is the result of students having choice in what they read and how much they read, of student engagement with books, and of increased time actually reading, and of students having the opportunity to talk about their reading with others and to reflect on their reading by writing. It is the effect of students behaving like real readers instead of being caught in "doing too much stuff" about reading.

The recognition of learning is, however, always more than the marks recorded in a grade book. Your observations of animated (grand) conversations, of thoughtful journal responses, of comprehension tasks where students demonstrate relationships among ideas, of all students (even the reluctant readers) choosing a book and sticking with it, ready to pounce on their next book, are the true marks of learning. These are the behaviors of powerful, enthusiastic readers well on their way to becoming lifelong readers, readers who read.

LITERATURE CIRCLES BOOK LISTS

The book lists presented here are collections that my colleagues and I have used recently, with success, with groups of students in literature circles. Some are arranged thematically, others are not, just as at times you will want to present books around a theme and at other times you will not. Generally, these are arranged by grade level, in most cases with combined grade classes. These lists are starter book lists and should be expanded as your students read through them. The success of any book list depends on the match between books and students. It is important that every student in your class have a book that she or he will be able to read and will be interested in reading, so these lists are offered as suggestions, not as prescriptions. Share them with your colleagues, refine them, add to them, and continually ask your students what books they like to read.

* denotes the easiest book in the list

GRADE 2

Series

At the Grade 2 level, it is often a good idea to present books in a series. The repetition of characters involved in a variety of adventures is a great help to young readers. With each book they read, students begin with more knowledge of the characters and a heightened sense of their next adventure.

Abbott, Tony. *Secrets of Droon*. New York: Scholastic, 2003.

Dadey, Debbie. *Bailey School Kids*. New York: Scholastic, 2004.

Danziger, Paula. *Amber Brown*. New York: G.P. Putnam's Sons, 2003.

Magic School Bus. New York: Scholastic, 2004. [various authors]

Osborne, Mary Pope. *The Magic Tree House.* New York: Random House, 1998.

Parish, Peggy. *Amelia Bedelia.* New York: Greenwillow Books, 1997.

Park, Barbara. *Junie B. Jones.* New York: Random House, 2002.

Peterson, John. *The Littles.* New York: Scholastic, 1968.

Warner, Gertrude. *Boxcar Children.* Morton Grove, IL: A. Whitman, 1997.

Publishers' Kits

Many publishing houses have kits containing a number of short novels that work well in literature circles. Two good ones are Nelson Language Arts: Supplementary Readers and Mammoth Storybooks.

Nelson Language Arts: Supplementary Readers

Cowley, Joy. *When the Truck Got Stuck.* Wellington, NZ: Learning Media, 1999.

Jewell, Nancy. *Two Silly Trolls.* New York: HarperCollins, 1992.

Wilson, Trevor. *Ducks Crossing.* Wellington, NZ: Learning Media, 1999.

Wishinsky, Frieda. *Give Maggie a Chance.* Markham, ON: Fitzhenry and Whiteside, 2002.

Mammoth Storybooks

Tomlinson, Jill. *The Owl Who Was Afraid of the Dark.* Cambridge, MA: Candlewick, 2001.

--- . *The Hen Who Wouldn't Give Up.* London: Egmont, 2004.

--- . *The Otter Who Wanted to Know.* London: Egmont, 2004.

GRADES 3 AND 4

A Collection Built by Two Teachers Team-Teaching

Cleary, Beverly. *Runaway Ralph.* New York: HarperTrophy, 2000.

DiCamillo, Kate. *Because of Winn Dixie.* Cambridge, MA: Candlewick, 2001.

--- . *The Tiger Rising.* Cambridge, MA: Candlewick, 2001.

Edmonds, Yvette. *Yuit.* Toronto: Napoleon, 1993.

Ehrlich, Gretel. *A Blizzard Year: Timmy's Almanac of the Seasons.* New York: Hyperion Books for Children, 1999.

l'Engle, Madeline. *A Wrinkle in Time.* New York: Bantam Doubleday Dell Books for Young Readers, 1962.

*Kinsey-Warnock, Natalie. *Canada Geese Quilt.* New York: Cobblehill Books-Dutton, 1989.

Tales of Children and Animals

Atwater, Richard, and Florence Atwater. *Mr. Popper's Penguins.* New York: Little, Brown, 1988.

Blume, Judy. *Tales of a Fourth Grade Nothing.* New York: Puffin, 1972.

--- . *Freckle Juice.* New York: Dell, 1986.

Dahl, Roald. *James and the Giant Peach.* New York: Puffin, 2001.

Davis, Deborah. *Secret of the Seal.* New York: Crown, 1989.

DiCamillo, Kate. *Because of Winn Dixie.* Cambridge, MA: Candlewick, 2001.

Osborne, Mary Pope. *Polar Bears Past Bedtime.* New York: Random House, 1998.

Smith, Doris Buchanan. *Taste of Blackberries.* New York: Crowell, 1973.

GRADES 4 AND 5

Adventure and Animal Stories

Bailey, Linda. *How Come the Best Clues Are Always in the Garbage?* Toronto: Kids Can, 1992.

Byars, Betsy. *Midnight Fox.* New York: Avon Books, 1968.

Horne, Constance. *Emily Carr's Woo.* Lantzville, BC: Oolichan, 1995.

Jungman, Ann. *Lucy Keeps the Wolf from the Door.* London: Collins, 1989.

Smucker, Barbara. *Jacob's Little Giant.* New York: Puffin, 1987.

Canadian Historical Fiction

There are several Canadian history series that are particularly popular for this age group: Our Canadian Girls Series (Toronto: Penguin); Adventure.net Series (Vancouver: Whitecap); Orca Young Reader Series (Victoria: Orca). This list includes at least one from each series.

*Citra, Becky. *Danger at the Landing.* Orca Young Reader Series. Victoria: Orca, 2002.

Harris, Dorothy. *Hobo Jungle.* Our Canadian Girls Series. Toronto: Penguin Books, 2002.

Kositsky, Lynne. *A Mighty Big Imagining.* Our Canadian Girls Series. Toronto: Penguin Books, 2001.

Lawson, Julie. *Across the James Bay Bridge.* Our Canadian Girls Series. Toronto: Penguin Books, 2001.

McKay, Sharon. *Terror in the Harbour.* Our Canadian Girls Series. Toronto: Penguin, 2001.

Spalding, Andrea, and David Spalding. *The Lost Sketch.* Adventure.net Series. Toronto: Whitecap, 1999.

Walters, Eric. *Camp X.* Toronto: Puffin Canada, 2003.

GRADES 4, 5, AND 6

All Families Have Challenges

Many schools teach social responsibility in an effort to increase students' senses of being cared about, which, in turn, decreases the number of bullying incidents among them. This collection treats the issues of solving problems in peaceful ways; valuing diversity and defending human rights; exercising democratic rights and responsibilities. Note that this list includes two picture books, which are meant to support the novels.

Baylor, Byrd. *The Table Where Rich People Sit.* Toronto: Maxwell Macmillan Canada, 1994. [picture book]

Butcher, Kristin. *The Gramma War.* Victoria: Orca, 2001.

DiCamillo, Kate. *Because of Winn Dixie.* Cambridge, MA: Candlewick, 2001.

Gantos, Jack. *Joey Pigza Loses Control.* New York: HarperTrophy, 2002.

Horvath, Polly. *Everything on a Waffle.* Toronto: Douglas and McIntyre, 2001.

Pearson, Kit. *Awake and Dreaming.* Toronto: Penguin, 1996.

Smith, Robert Kimmel. *The War with Grandpa.* New York: Delacorte, 1984.

Tan, Shaun. *The Red Tree.* Vancouver: Simply Read Books, 2002. [picture book]

GRADES 5 AND 6

Students in Grades 5 and 6 are beginning to delve into books about difficult choices. This list is designed for children moving into the larger world, coming of age, gaining responsibility, and learning about their own capabilities.

Ellis, Deborah. *The Breadwinner.* Toronto: Douglas and McIntyre, 2000.

--- . *Parvana's Journey.* Toronto: Douglas and McIntyre, 2002.

Korman, Gordon. *Island, Book 1: Shipwreck.* New York: Scholastic, 2001. [a three-book series]

Paterson, Katherine. *Bridge to Terabithia.* New York: Crowell, 1977.

Sachar, Louis. *Holes.* New York: Farrar, Straus and Giroux, 1998.

Watts, Irene N. *Good-bye Marianne.* Toronto: Tundra Books, 1998.

--- . *Remember Me.* Toronto: Tundra, 2000.

GRADES 6 AND 7

Hope, Courage, Survival, Persecution, the Power of Family

At the Grade 6 and 7 level, students often request novels about personal challenges. The books in this collection have been very popular.

Boraks-Nemetz, Lillian. *The Old Brown Suitcase.* Brentwood Bay, BC: Ben-Simon, 1994.

*Kidd, Diana. *Onion Tears.* New York: Orchard, 1989.

Little, Jean. *Willow and Twig.* Toronto: Puffin Canada, 2001.

Matas, Carol. *Jesper.* Markham, ON: Scholastic Canada, 1989.

--- . *Daniel's Story.* New York: Scholastic, 1993.

*Propp, Vera W. *When the Soldiers Were Gone.* New York: Putnam's, 1999.

Watkins, Yoko Kawashima, and Jean Fritz. *So Far from the Bamboo Grove.* New York: Lothrop, Lee and Shepard, 1986.

Whelan, Gloria. *Good-bye, Vietnam.* New York: Knopf, 1992.

Fantasy

Avi. *Perloo the Bold.* New York: Scholastic, 1998.

Bruchac, Joseph. *Skeleton Man.* New York: HarperCollins, 2001.

Coville, Bruce. *The Monster's Ring.* New York: Pocket Books, 1982.

Kilworth, Garry. *Spiggot's Quest.* London: Atom, 2002.

Rodda, Emily. *The Forests of Silence.* New York: Scholastic, 2001.

Stewart, Paul. *Beyond the Deep Woods.* London: Corgi, 1998.

Heroes

Of particular interest in this collection is the pairing of *War Horse* and *Farm Boy,* essentially the same story told from different points of view.

Gavin, Jamila. *Blood Stone.* London: Egmont, 2003. [favorite]

Hooper, Mary. *At the Sign of the Sugared Plum.* London: Bloomsbury, 2003.

*Morpurgo, Michael. *War Horse.* London: Egmont, 1982. [If you purchase two copies of *Farm Boy* and four copies of *War Horse,* these choices can be used for one discussion group: same author, same character, different reading levels.]

--- . *Farm Boy.* London: Pavilion, 1997.

Van Draanen, Wendelin. *Flipped.* New York: Knopf, 2001. [favorite]

Withers, Pam. *Raging River.* North Vancouver: Walrus, 2003.

Yee, Paul. *The Bone Collector's Son.* Vancouver: Tradewind Books, 2003.

GRADE 8

Making historical fiction available for literature circles reinforces the social studies and/or humanities curricula. The Middle Ages is a popular historical period in Grade 8.

Avi. *Crispin: The Cross of Lead.* New York: Hyperion Paperbacks for Children, 2004.

Blackwood, Gary. *The Shakespeare Stealer.* New York: Puffin Books, 1998.

--- . *Shakespeare's Scribe.* New York: Dutton Children's Books, 2000.

Bradford, Karleen. *There Will Be Wolves.* Toronto: HarperCollins, 1992.

*Bulla, Clyde Robert. *The Sword in the Tree.* New York: HarperTrophy, 2000.

Cushman, Karen. *The Midwife's Apprentice.* New York: HarperCollins, 1995.

Harnett, Cynthia. *The Load of the Unicorn.* Cleveland: World, 1960.

Hooper, Mary. *At the Sign of the Sugared Plum.* London: Bloomsbury, 2003.

Jinks, Catherine. *Pagan's Crusade.* Sydney: Hodder and Stoughton, 1993.

Morpurgo, Michael. *The Sleeping Sword.* London: Egmont, 2002.

*Platt, Richard. *Castle Diary: The Journal of Tobias Burgess.* Cambridge, MA: Candlewick, 1999.

Yolen, Jane, and Robert J. Harris. *Girl in a Cage.* New York: Philomel Books, 2002.

--- . *Sword of the Rightful King.* Orlando: Harcourt, 2004.

GRADES 8 AND 9

Not all books in literature circles are linked thematically. This collection is simply a collection of good reads.

Bauer, Joan. *Hope Was Here.* New York: G.P. Putnam's Sons, 2000.

Cabot, Meg [formerly Jenny Carroll]. *1-800-Where-R-You.* Simon and Shuster Children's Books, 2002-04. [series]

Crutcher, Chris. *Crazy Horse Electric Game.* New York: HarperTempest, 1987.

Gibbons, Alan. *Caught in the Crossfire.* London: Orion Children's Books, 2003.

Haddam, Jane. *Skeleton Key.* New York: St. Martin's Paperbacks, 2000.

Howe, Norma. *The Adventures of the Blue Avenger.* New York: HarperTempest, 2000.

*Nix, Garth. *Mister Monday.* Markham, ON: Scholastic Canada, 2003.

GRADE 9

Making historical fiction available for literature circles reinforces the social studies and/or humanities curricula. The Industrial Revolution is a popular historical period in Grade 9.

Aiken, Joan. *Midnight Is a Place.* New York: Viking, 1974.

Almond, David. *Kit's Wilderness.* New York: Laurel-Leaf, 2001.

D'Adamo, Francesco. *Iqbal.* New York: Atheneum Books for Young Readers, 2001.

Dickens, Charles. *Oliver Twist.* Ed. Lesley Baxter. Illus. Michael Morpurgo. New York: Dial Books, 1996. [You could use this or the original edition.]

Doherty, Berlie. *The Street Child.* New York: Orchard Books, 1994.

Heneghan, James. *The Grave.* Vancouver: Douglas and McIntyre, 2000.

Holeman, Linda. *Search of the Moon King's Daughter.* Toronto: Tundra Books, 2002.

Holman, Sheri. *The Dress Lodger.* New York: Atlantic Monthly Press, 2000.

Laird, Elizabeth. *The Garbage King.* London: Macmillan Children's Books, 2003.

*Matas, Carol. *Rosie in New York City—Gotcha!* Toronto: Key Porter Books, 2003.

*Wallace, Barbara Brooks. *Sparrows in the Scullery.* New York: Atheneum Books for Young Readers, 1997.

GRADES 8, 9, AND 10

Pulling Strength from Within

In an effort to resolve their personal problems, adolescents often indulge in a form of bibliotherapy, in which they read about others with challenges similar to their own problems. The books in this list have been chosen to connect with the following social responsibility strands: solving problems in peaceful ways; valuing diversity and defending human rights; exercising democratic rights and responsibilities. Note that this list includes two picture books, which are meant to support the novels.

Ellis, Deborah. *Looking for X.* Toronto: Douglas and McIntyre, 1999.

--- . *The Heaven Shop.* Markham, ON: Fitzhenry and Whiteside, 2004.

Fleischman, Paul. *Whirligig.* New York: Laurel-Leaf Books, 1998.

*Laird, Elizabeth. *Secret Friends.* London: Hodder Children's Books, 1996.

Madonna. *Mr. Peabody's Apples.* New York: Callaway, 2003. [picture book]

Maguire, Gregory. *The Good Liar.* New York: Clarion Books, 1999.

Mikaelsen, Ben. *Touching Spirit Bear.* New York: HarperCollins, 2001.

Morpurgo, Michael. *Private Peaceful.* London: Collins, 2004.

Muth, Jon J. *The Three Questions.* New York: Scholastic, 2002. [picture book]

GRADES 10 AND 11

Making historical fiction available for literature circles reinforces the social studies and/or humanities curricula. War novels are popular among Grade 10 and 11 students. Note that this list includes a number of picture books, which are meant to support the novels.

Craddock, Sonia. *Sleeping Boy.* Illus. Leonid Gore. New York: Atheneum Books for Young Readers, 1999. [picture book]

Findley, Timothy. *The Wars.* Toronto: Clarke, Irwin, 1977.

Foreman, Michael. *War Boy.* New York: Arcade, 1989. [WWI picture book]

--- . *War Game.* New York: Arcade, 1994. [WWI picture book]

Hughes, Dean. *Soldier Boys.* New York: Atheneum, 2001.

Kogawa, Joy. *Obasan.* Toronto: Penguin Books, 1981.

Morpurgo, Michael. *Private Peaceful.* London: Collins, 2004. [WWI]

Remarque, Erich Maria. *All Quiet on the Western Front.* Philadelphia: Chelsea House, 2001.

Spiegelman, Art. *Maus.* New York: Pantheon Books, 1991. [picture book]

GRADE 12

Novels for Communications Courses

Alphin, Elaine. *Counterfeit Son.* San Diego: Harcourt, 2000.

Brooks, Martha. *True Confessions of a Heartless Girl.* Toronto: Douglas and McIntyre, 2002.

Gibbons, Alan. *The Edge.* London: Orion Children's Books, 2002.

Howe, Norma. *The Adventures of Blue Avenger.* New York: HarperTempest, 2000.

Myers, Walter Dean. *Monster.* New York: HarperCollins, 1999.

Spinelli, Jerry. *Stargirl.* New York: Alfred A. Knopf, 2002.

Staples, Suzanne. *Shabanu, Daughter of the Wind.* New York: Dell Laurel-Leaf, 1989.

Novels for Literature Courses

Atwood, Margaret. *The Handmaid's Tale.* Toronto: Seal Books, 1985.

Huxley, Aldous. *Brave New World.* New York: Perennial Classics, 1932.

Orwell, George. *Nineteen Eighty-Four.* London: Secker and Warburg, 1949.

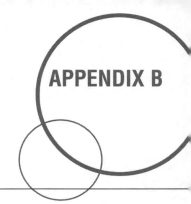

BIBLIOGRAPHY

CHILDREN'S BOOKS REFERRED TO IN THE TEXT
(excluding those books found in Appendix A)

Baglio, Ben. *Pup at the Palace.* New York: Scholastic Paperbacks, 2003.

Collier, J.L., and C. Collier. *Jump Ship to Freedom.* New York, Delacorte Press, 1981.

Dahl, Roald. *Charlie and the Chocolate Factory.* New York: Puffin, 1998.

Greenwood, Barbara. *The Last Safe House.* Toronto: Kids Can Press, 1998.

Gregory, Kristiana. *Cleopatra VII: Daughter of the Nile.* The Royal Diaries Series. New York: Scholastic, 1999.

Haskens, Jim. *Get on Board: The Story of the Underground Railroad.* New York: Scholastic, 1993.

Heneghan, James. *Torn Away.* Victoria: Orca Books, 2003.

Howe, Deborah, and James Howe. *Bunnicula: A Rabbit-Tale of Mystery.* New York: Aladdin, 1996.

Hopkinson, Deborah. *Sweet Clara and the Freedom Quilt.* New York: Knopf, 1993.

Korman, Gordon. *Liar, Liar, Pants on Fire.* New York: Scholastic, 1997.

Kositsky, Lynne. *Rachel: A Mighty Big Imagining.* Our Canadian Girls Series 1. Toronto: Penguin Books, 2001.

*--- . *The Maybe House.* Our Canadian Girls Series 2. Toronto: Penguin Books, 2002.

Lester, Julius. *From Slave Ship to Freedom Road.* New York: Dial Books, 1998.

Lowry, Lois. *The Giver.* New York: Laurel Leaf, 1994.

Lyons, Mary E. *Letters from a Slave Girl.* Toronto: Maxwell MacMillan Canada, 1992. [challenging]

McCammon, Robert. *A Boy's Life.* New York: Pocket Books, 1991.

Paterson, Katherine. *The Great Gilly Hopkins.* New York: HarperTrophy, 1987.

--- . *Jip: His Story.* New York: Puffin Books, 1998.

Paulsen, Gary. *Sarny: A Life Remembered.* New York: Delacorte Press, 1997. [challenging]

Ringgold, Faith. *Aunt Harriet's Underground Railroad in the Sky.* New York: Crown Publishers, 1992. [picture book, fiction]

Silverstein, Shel. *The Missing Piece.* New York: HarperCollins, 1976.

Stinson, Kathy. *Marie-Claire: Dark Spring.* Our Canadian Girls Series. Toronto: Penguin Books, 2001.

Winters, Jeanette. *Follow the Drinking Gourd.* New York: Knopf, 1988.

ACADEMIC SOURCES REFERRED TO IN THE TEXT

British Columbia Ministry of Education. *Enhancing and Evaluating Oral Communication in the Secondary Grades.* Victoria: Ministry of Education, 1998.

---. *B.C. Performance Standards for Reading Literature.* Victoria: Ministry of Education, 2000. www.bced.gov.bc.ca

Brownlie, Faye, Catherine Feniak, and Vicki McCarthy. *Instruction and Assessment of ESL Learners.* Winnipeg: Portage and Main Press, 2004.

Brownlie, F., S. Close, and L. Wingren. *Reaching for Higher Thought.* Scarborough, ON: Nelson Canada, 1988.

Brownlie, F., and C. Feniak. *Student Diversity.* Markham, ON: Pembroke, 1998.

Brownlie, F., and J. King. *Learning in Safe Schools.* Markham, ON: Pembroke, 2000.

Fielding, Linda, and David Pearson. "Reading Comprehension: What Works." *Education Leadership* 51.5 (February 1994).

Harste, J., K. Short, and C. Burke. *Creating Classrooms for Authors: The Reading-Writing Connection.* Portsmouth, NH: Heinemann, 1989.

Harvey, Stephanie. *Nonfiction Matters.* York, ME: Stenhouse, 1998.

Literacy in the Middle Years, Part 2. www.insinc.com/ministryofeducation/20041118> [webcast]

Santa, Carol. *Content Reading Including Study Systems.* Dubuque, IA: Kendall Hunt, 1991.

Wells, Gordon. *The Meaning Makers: Children Learning Language and Using Language to Learn.* Portsmouth, NH: Heinemann, 1986.